The Government Inspector

Nikola Gogol was born in 1809. His comedy about a penniless clerk from Moscow who is mistaken for a government inspector by the corrupt officials of a small town in Tsarist Russia was first staged in 1836. It was widely taken as a satire on the corruption of Russian officialdom. Thanks partly to Pushkin's efforts it was passed by the censor, and the Tsar, accepting it on the level of farce, gave it his blessing. Though satire is an element in the play, it is the wild inventiveness of Gogol's comic fantasy that has ensured the play's survival as one of the great comedies of mistaken identity. This comedy of innocent corruption has a direct appeal to modern audiences as a hilarious study in and celebration of the grotesque and absurd elements in human nature.

The photograph on the front cover shows Paul Scofield and Paul Rogers in the Royal Shakespeare Company's production at the Aldwych Theatre. Photo: David Sim, reproduced by courtesy of The Observer. *The picture on the back cover is reproduced by courtesy of the Radio Times Hulton Picture Library.*

Methuen's Theatre Classics

NIKOLAI GOGOL

THE GOVERNMENT
INSPECTOR

an English version by
EDWARD O. MARSH & JEREMY BROOKS

EYRE METHUEN LTD
11 NEW FETTER LANE LONDON EC4

*This translation first published in 1968 by
Methuen & Co Ltd, 11 New Fetter Lane, London EC4
© 1968 Edward O. Marsh and Jeremy Brooks
Reprinted 1972, 1973 and 1975 by Eyre Methuen Ltd.
ISBN 0 413 30990 8*

Printed Offset Litho in Great Britain by
COX & WYMAN LTD., FAKENHAM, NORFOLK

Nikolai Vassilyevich Gogol

20 March 1809	Born in Sorochintsy in the province of Poltava.
1828	Graduated from school and went to St Petersburg.
1829	Published poems *Italy* and *Hanz Kuechelgarten*. Entered Civil Service.
1831	Left Civil Service, began teaching history at a young ladies' institute. Met Pushkin (1799–1837). Published first volume of *Evenings on a Farm near Dikanka*.
1832	Published second volume of *Evenings on a Farm near Dikanka*.
1834	Appointed Reader in World History at St Petersburg University.
1835	Published two volumes of stories entitled *Mirgorod*, and *Arabesques*, a collection of essays and stories (including *Diary of a Madman*). Wrote two plays, *Marriage* and *The Government Inspector*.
December 1835	Resigned post at University.
19 April 1836	Premiere of *The Government Inspector* at the Alexandrinsky Theatre, St Petersburg.
25 May 1836	First Moscow performance of *The Government Inspector* at the Maly Theatre.
June 1836	Left St Petersburg for Germany.

October 1836	Switzerland. Began writing *Dead Souls*.
Winter 1836–37	Paris.
March 1837	To Rome.
Winter 1839–40	Returned to Russia.
May 1840	Back to Italy via Vienna.
Winter 1841–42	In Russia. Finished his short story, *The Overcoat*.
1842	Published First Part of *Dead Souls*. Published revised version of *The Government Inspector*. Published *Marriage*.
9 December	Premiere of *Marriage* at Alexandrinsky Theatre, St Petersburg.
1842–48	Travelled around Western Europe, trying unsuccessfully to complete *Dead Souls*.
1843	First collected edition of Gogol's works.
1845	Burnt uncompleted second volume of *Dead Souls*.
1846	Tried unsuccessfully to publish epilogue to *The Government Inspector*. Resumed *Dead Souls*.
1848	Pilgrimage to Palestine. Returned to Russia.
21 February 1852	Died in Moscow as a result of primitive medical treatment and self-imposed starvation whilst his mind was unbalanced by religious guilt.

Introduction

Nikolai Gogol was born in 1809, the son of a landowner in the little Ukrainian town of Sorochintsy. He left school in 1828 and went to St Petersburg where he entered the Civil Service at the fourteenth and lowest grade. Soon bored with the drudgery of a clerk's existence and appalled by the colossal expense of keeping up appearances in the capital, he decided to seek a more remunerative profession. Encouraged by his earlier successes in school theatricals he auditioned at the Imperial Theatre, but his stunted appearance and huge pointed nose were ill-suited to the tragic roles he offered, and he was a ludicrous failure.

Next he tried writing, but the two idyllic poems which he published were ridiculed by those few critics who did not ignore them completely. So dismayed was he, that he bought up all copies of the second poem and destroyed them. Eventually he secured a post as teacher of history in a young ladies' institute, and then shortly afterwards gained his first success as a writer. Taking advantage of the prevailing taste for tales of provincial life, he published in 1831 the first volume of *Evenings on a Farm near Dikanka*, a collection of short stories set in his native Ukraine. The work was well received in literary circles and he was encouraged to write further; he extended his range to include Hoffmanesque fantasies, historical and critical essays, stories of Petersburg life and the psychological study, *Diary of a Madman* (1835).

In 1834, with the help of his literary friends, Gogol became Reader in World History at Petersburg University. Mere eloquence quickly proved insufficient to hide his thin knowledge of the subject, and he soon resorted to pictorial aids and a feigned toothache to eke out his lectures. After sixteen months the appointment was terminated to mutual relief. Gogol may be pardoned this neglect of his pedagogical duties, for his literary output was growing fast; during his time as a university lecturer he published two volumes of essays and short stories, and wrote two full-length plays. The first of these was a domestic farce called *Marriage*, which anticipates the style of Chekhov's one-act farces; the second was *The Government Inspector*.

The Russian dramatic stage of the 1830's presented a picture of unrelieved Philistinism. The public was offered a choice between extravagantly staged historical romances, lurid melodrama or crude vaudeville, and playgoing was no more than an empty social diversion. Genuine Russian masterpieces like Pushkin's *Boris Godunov* (1825) and Lermontov's *Masquerade* (1835) were suppressed by a pathologically suspicious censor and were destined to wait over thirty years for their first public performances. *Woe from Wit* (1823), Griboyedov's masterly denunciation of Moscow society, was performed only in grossly mutilated form until 1869.

Whereas Gogol had conceived *Marriage* as pure farce, his intention with *The Government Inspector* was altogether more ambitious. Condemning the cheap sensations of the melodrama and the irrelevant trivialities of the vaudeville, he sought with his comedy to bring out the significance of everyday happenings. Much as he admired the satirical force and technical brilliance of Molière and Beaumarchais, he rejected their decorum, their refined dialogue, their traditional characters. Modern drama, he asserted, must reflect the problems of modern society, and comedy must help us to acknowledge our vices and shortcomings by exposing them to ridicule. With a typically naïve disregard for the furore his observations on society were sure to cause, he had faith in the purifying and elevating power of laughter.

It was Pushkin who suggested to Gogol the theme of mistaken identity for his play, having been mistaken himself for an itinerant government snooper in Nizhny Novgorod. But in any case it was a common enough anecdote, and Gogol is believed to have based the character of Khlyestakov on a Petersburg publisher, who was a notorious pathological liar and had once posed successfully as an inspector in Bessarabia.

His imagination fired, Gogol wrote *The Government Inspector* in the last three months of 1835. The play shows how far he succeeded in breaking free from the conventions which he had condemned, although it should be noted that the original version of the text (which was the only one to be performed until 1888) contained many elements of pure farce which in later versions Gogol gradually eliminated. It may be argued that such situations as the confrontation between Anna Andreyevna and Khlyestakov, after she has discovered him kissing her daughter, and the traditional letter dénouement reveal Gogol's debt to French classical models, but mostly we are in the realm of an altogether new and more robust theatre far more closely related to life itself.

In the Russian theatre of the 1830's the stage director was concerned with little more than ensuring that the actors did not actually collide on stage. Gogol, however demonstrated a quite unprecedented concern over the production of his play, going so far as to demand full company rehearsals in the presence of the director. He placed particular emphasis on the final tableau, insisting that each pose should suggest an individual reaction appropriate to the person's character. His instructions to the actors could easily have come from Stanislavsky a hundred years later: 'Before seizing on the insignificant oddities and external peculiarities of the character, the intelligent actor should strive to grasp first the universal significance of his rôle . . .'

Khlyestakov he characterized as 'a young man of twenty-three – slender, not to say thin. He tends to be rather silly, to the extent even, as the saying goes, of being "not quite all there" – the sort of person his fellow workers in the same office consider to be a dead loss. He speaks and acts without a thought for anything or anybody. He is quite incapable of giving his undivided attention to any single idea. His speech is convulsive, the words jerk out in a totally unexpected fashion. The more simple and ingenuous the actor can appear in this part the better he will be. Khlyestakov dresses very fashionably.'[1]

Thanks partly to Pushkin's efforts, the play was passed by

[1] see p. 15.

the censor and received its first performance on 19th April, 1836, at the Alexandrinsky Theatre in St Petersburg. For Gogol it was a twofold disaster. In spite of all precautions, his minutely observed characters and exactly calculated *coups de théâtre* were debased to crude farce by an insensitive director and cast. Khlyestakov, protested Gogol, was played as 'a stock swindler, a typical vaudeville rogue'. Tsar Nicholas, a monarch not noted for his critical acumen, accepted the play on this level, was vastly amused, and commanded the Royal Family and his ministers to see it. But this did not stop conservative opinion from rising up in protest at what it took to be calculated subversion.

In vain did Gogol plead that his intention was moral rather than social satire, that the true inspector's arrival implied the reassertion of the moral rectitude of the State over the more flexible standards of its functionaries. The State's functionaries were not to be placated; indeed they were further incensed by those liberal critics who hailed Gogol as the harbinger of a new era of critical realism. For the rest of the season the play was performed almost every second day, but its unabating *succès de scandale* proved too much for Gogol's reticent spirit and in June 1836 he fled the country to return only occasionally over the next twelve years.

Gogol continued to work on *The Government Inspector*, seeking to eradicate the farcical elements which he felt had led to the burlesque of the original production. In 1842 he published the revised version which was not performed until 1888, but which has become accepted since as canonical[1]. By this time he had come to recognize in the play what others had seen from the start; indeed, he barbed its sting with such additions as the Mayor's direct address to the audience and the reference to 'those writers, damned snivelling liberals' in the final scene – to say nothing of the epigraph: 'Don't blame the mirror if your face is lopsided . . .'

During the final ten years of his life, up to his death in 1852, Gogol was obsessed with the evangelical mission of reforming Russia through the medium of literature. It was this which

[1] The version which follows is based on this edition.

made him transform his novel *Dead Souls* from a hilarious picaresque fantasy into a scarcely credible vision of an Arcadian Russia inhabited by masters and serfs in blissful coexistence. It was never completed and much of it he destroyed in frantic despair.

Just as abortively he wrote a new version of *The Government Inspector*, adding an epilogue in which the dramatis personae appear and explain that the play is really a religious allegory with the townspeople representing our earthly passions and the true Inspector the Divine Inquisitor. This ill-conceived appendage was neither published nor staged, thanks to Gogol's friends who rejected it as one further product of his mystical delusions.

The Government Inspector has been performed constantly in Russia for the past 130 years, and since its first performance abroad in Paris in 1853 it has held its place in the international repertoire. The play's construction is foolproof enough for it to work splendidly as pure knockabout farce, but it is Gogol's mastery of the grotesque, a grotesque rooted in his unsparing observation of living people, which makes the work sublimest comedy and a supreme theatrical challenge.

EDWARD BRAUN

Translators' Note

This version of *The Government Inspector* was prepared especially for the Royal Shakespeare Company's production at the Aldwych Theatre in January 1966. The play is set in a small provincial town in the heart of Russia, far from St Petersburg and Moscow. This distance from the capitals is important. As the Mayor says, 'You could gallop for three years without reaching a foreign country'. It is this sense of the vast distances between themselves and any centre of authority which gives the officials of Gogol's town a feeling of security from outside interference, and allows them to administer the town as corruptly and inefficiently as they like; and makes it inevitable that even the lowliest clerk from St Petersburg should seem, in their eyes, to glow with sophistication, wit and authority.

It is essential, therefore, that the speech of the officials and townspeople should have a distinctly provincial flavour, to contrast with the acquired polish which Khlyestakov has picked up in the capital. In order to avoid the inevitable 'Mummerset' which tends to emerge when actors are asked to produce an unspecified country accent, Peter Hall, the director, decided to imagine the play as being set in a remote East Anglian village. Suffolk and Norfolk are, in fact, not all that far from London, but they nevertheless do have a curious sense of remoteness from 'civilization'; and the rhythms and vowel sounds of East Anglian speech are so distinctive that there seemed a fair chance of our being able to impose some cohesion on the accents used by the cast. We had a tape, made from B.B.C. recordings, of East Anglian dialect stories, which was repeatedly played over to the cast during rehearsals; and expert coaching from two East Anglians – Donald Burton and Peter Hall.

This tape was also used in preparing the text. The starting

point was Edward Marsh's original translation from the Russian, which was then adapted as far as possible to fit the rhythms and speech patterns of our chosen dialect. In the case of the two visitors from the capital, we imagined Ossip as a cockney water-rat, Khlyestakov as a suburban dandy with pretensions above his station. This is not quite faithful to the Russian text, since both Khlyestakov and his servant originally came from a country province even more remote than the one they are now passing through; but it is not possible, in England, to 'place' them with the same social accuracy if they are also given a provincial accent.

The Russian custom, unfamiliar to our ears, of using the patronymic as well as the Christian name in ordinary conversation was to some extent made easier to deal with by contraction, so that 'Amos Fyodorovich' became 'Amos Fy'do'vich', and 'Artemy Philipovich' became 'Art'y Ph'lip'ich'. These contracted forms which do not necessarily correspond to actual Russian abbreviations, are given, in parentheses in the cast list, together with the adapted versions of some of the names which were used in this production. The justification for also changing many of the surnames – 'Lyapkin-Tyapkin into 'Flapkin-Slapkin', 'Khlopov' into 'Plopov', is that most of Gogol's names have, in Russian, either a direct or an onomatopoeic joke-meaning. The civil ranks which we have attributed to the town's officials are a necessary invention. In nineteenth-century Russia, official society was divided into a seemingly infinite gradation of ranks – one of the proliferations of Tsarist bureaucracy which Gogol was always attacking – but a direct transcript of these into English would be either meaningless or misleading.

Textual cuts which were found necessary for the Aldwych production in the course of rehearsals have been indicated by enclosing the cut passages in square brackets. A small number of textual additions were made (including a fairly liberal sprinkling of Russian proverbs) but all of these, save one, have been removed from the present text. The exception, which seems a necessary clarification of the action, has been put in bold brackets (p. 53).

NOTES BY GOGOL ON
CHARACTERS AND COSTUMES

THE MAYOR. His hair has turned grey in the government service but in his way he is far from being a fool. He takes bribes but still manages to keep a certain measure of dignity. He is quite a serious person, something of a moralist, in fact. What he says is never too much, never too little; when he does speak it is never too loud, never too soft, and yet his every word is heavy with meaning. His features are as coarse and cruel as those of any successful person who has begun at the bottom in a difficult service. He veers rapidly from fear to joy, from subservience to arrogance, as befits a man with scarcely developed spiritual feelings. He is normally dressed in the frock-coat of his official uniform, of which the most striking features are the buttons and button-holes. In addition to this he wears spurred and highly-polished jack-boots. His hair is short and grizzled.

ANNA ANDREYEVNA, the Mayor's wife, is a provincial coquette, not exactly old yet, whose education has been about equally divided between romantic novels and anthology verse. Her main concerns are the pantry and the servants. She is extremely in-quisitive and her vanity is displayed at every turn. She now and then gets the upper hand of her husband simply because he is not ready with an answer. She uses this power only for trivial things, however, lecturing him and sneering at him turn and turn about. She has four complete changes of costume during the play.

KHLYESTAKOV, a young man of twenty-three – slender, not to say thin. He tends to be rather silly, to the extent even, as the saying goes, of being 'not quite all there' – the sort of person his fellow workers in the same office consider a dead loss. He speaks and acts without a thought for anything or anybody. He is quite incapable of giving his undivided attention to any single idea. His speech is convulsive, the words jerk out in a totally un-expected fashion. The more simple and ingenuous the actor can appear in this part the better he will be. Khlyestakov dresses very fashionably.

OSSIP, Khlyestakov's servant, is rather like all servants who are getting on in years – serious in manner, eyes usually downcast, a moralizer given to treating himself to sermons he really means for his master. His voice is normally quite flat and smooth – though when talking to his master he can be rough and abrupt to the point of rudeness. He is more intelligent than his master and so he grasps things more rapidly, but he is not very willing to talk and, being a rascal into the bargain, prefers to keep his own counsel. He wears a long, grey or blue jacket, visibly threadbare.

BOBCHINSKY and DOBCHINSKY, two landowners, of the breed that would rather live in town than on their estates. Both are short and squat and very inquisitive. They are extraordinarily alike. They both chatter rather than speak, helping their words along with hand-waving and gesticulation. Dobchinsky is slightly the taller and more serious of the two, Bobchinsky jollier and livelier.

LYAPKIN-TYAPKIN, the Judge. A man who has read five or six books and who consequently inclines to freethinking. He is a great one for conjecture and as a result his every word has an air of profundity. The actor playing the part must keep a look of deep significance throughout and he must always speak in an exaggerated drawl, sounding rather like those grandfather clocks that strain and hiss before they strike.

ZEMLYANIKA, the Charity Commissioner, is a stout, clumsy, cumbersome man, who is nevertheless a wily rascal. He is most anxious to oblige and is very fussy.

THE POSTMASTER is so simple that he can only be called naïve.

The other parts call for no special comment. Their originals are in any case always with us.

The cast should be specially attentive to the concluding tableau. The final speech, from the Gendarme, must stun everybody on stage, immediately and simultaneously, like an electric shock. The entire company should shift and freeze its position in a single instant. An exclamation of astonishment must be given by all the female characters simultaneously, as it were from a single pair of lungs. If this business is not properly performed the whole effect may be ruined.

Don't blame the mirror if your

face is lopsided.

— *popular saying*

This translation of The Government Inspector *was first performed by the Royal Shakespeare Company on 19th January, 1966, at the Aldwych Theatre with the following cast:*

THE MAYOR, Antòn Antònovich Skvoznìk Dmukhanòvsky (*Civil Mayor Second Class, Anton Ant'n'ich*)	Paul Rogers
THE JUDGE, Amos Fyòdorovich Lyàpkin-Tyàpkin (*Civil Captain First Class, Amos Fy'do'vich Flapkin-Slapkin*)	Brewster Mason
THE CHARITY COMMISSIONER, Artèmy Philìpovich Zemlyanìka (*Civil Captain Third Class, Art'y Ph'lip'ich Zemolina*)	Paul Hardwick
THE SCHOOLS SUPERINTENDENT, Lukà Lukìch Khlòpov (*Civil Officer Second Class, Luna Lunich Plopov*)	David Waller
THE POSTMASTER, Ivàn Kuzmìch Shpyòkin (*Civil Officer Sixth Class, Ivan Goosmich Myopik*)	David Warner
THE DISTRICT PHYSICIAN, Christiàn Ivànovich Hùbner (*Civil Officer Seventh Class*)	Terence Greenidge
THE POLICE INSPECTOR, Lieutenant Stefàn Ilyich Ukhovyòrtov (*Stepan Bullbich*)	Ted Valentine
PETER IVÀNOVICH BÒBCHINSKY, a Landowner	Tim Wylton
PETER IVÀNOVICH DÒBCHINSKY, a Landowner	Charles Kay

IVÀN ALEXÀNDROVICH KHLYESTAKÒV a Government Clerk from St Petersburg	Paul Scofield
ÒSSIP, his servant	Eric Porter
ANNA ANDRÈYEVNA, the Mayor's Wife	Patience Collier
MARIA ANTÒNOVNA, the Mayor's Daughter	Patsy Byrne
THE LOCKSMITH'S WIFE	Pamela Buchner
THE SERGEANT'S WIDOW	Estelle Kohler
KORÒBKIN'S WIFE	Madoline Thomas
SCHOOLS SUPERINTENDENT'S WIFE	Frances de la Tour
ABDÙLLIN, a Shopkeeper (*Abd'in*)	Donald Burton
MÌSHKA, the Mayor's Servant	John Kane
A WAITER, at the Inn	Timothy West
A GENDARME, from St Petersburg	Stanley Lebor

FYÒDOR ANDRÈYEVICH LYULYUKÒV (*Lulukov*)		Paul Starr
	Retired Officials	
IVÀN LÀZAREVICH RASTAKÒVSKY		Jonathan Hales
STEPÀN IVÀNOVICH KORÒBKIN		Timothy West
SVISTUNÒV (*Fistov*)		Jeffery Dench
PÙGOVITZIN (*Pushov*)	Police Constables	
DYERZHIMÒRDA (*Dustov*)		John Corvin

Shopkeepers, Guests, Townspeople, Petitioners

Directed by Peter Hall
Designed by John Bury and Elizabeth Duffield

Act One

SCENE ONE

A room in the MAYOR's *house. On stage are assembled the* CHARITY COMMISSIONER, *the* SCHOOLS SUPERINTENDENT, *the* JUDGE, *the* DISTRICT PHYSICIAN *and the* MAYOR.

MAYOR. [Well, gentlemen! I've asked you all here today because] I've got some very nasty news for you. [It looks as if] there's a Government Inspector on his way to see us.

JUDGE. On his way . . . *here*?

CHARITY COMMISSIONER. A Government Inspector?

MAYOR. A Government Inspector from Petersburg. Under secret orders. And travelling – incognito!

JUDGE. That's terrible!

CHARITY COMMISSIONER. Dear God, what'll become of us!

SCHOOLS SUPERINTENDENT. And under secret orders [too!]

MAYOR. I knew something horrible was going to happen. I was warned. I had this dream, last night, about these rats. Huge black fellers, [they were,] I never seen such rats in my life. In they come, two of them, very slow . . . creeping closer and closer all night through. Then they give a horrifying sniff – and turn tail and walk off. And this morning, there was this letter from Chmikhov – (*To the* CHARITY COMMISSIONER.) – you know him, Artemy Philipovich. Listen to this, now. 'Dear Friend and Bene- factor' (*He mumbles, skipping through it.*) '. . . want to . . . tell you . . . five hundred roubles . . . hasten to . . .' Ah! here we are, 'and hasten to warn you that a Government official is on his way to inspect the province, and our district in par- ticular. I have this from an absolutely reliable source. This Inspector is travelling incognito . . . (*He looks up.*) – in- cog-*nito-o* d'you see? – (*He reads.*) – and introduces himself under a different name in each district. I know that you, like everyone else, have your little weaknesses, you're much too sensible to say no to the perquisites of your office . . .' (*He coughs and looks around.*) Yes, well, we're all friends here . . . '. . . so I advise you to take every precaution you can, as he may turn up at any moment – if, indeed, he isn't already living among you – incognito! My sister Anna Kirilovna and her husband are staying with us. Ivan Kirilovich has put on a lot of weight and never stops playing the fiddle . . .' Yes, well, the rest of it's just family matters, d'you see . . . There you are. Now you know.

JUDGE. [This is incredible! What's it all about?

SCHOOLS SUPERINTENDENT. Yes, Anton Antonovich,] why should they want to inspect *us*?

MAYOR. It's the whim of fate, my friends. So far it's always been other districts, but our luck's changed now!

JUDGE. Anton Antonovich, it's my belief there's more to it than that. It's a political move, that is. It's my belief there's going to be a war, and they're sending an Inspector round to look for traitors!

MAYOR. War? Traitors? What are you talking about? This isn't a frontier town, is it? You could gallop for three years without reaching a foreign country.

JUDGE. You're wrong, Anton Antonovich. The authorities in Petersburg and Moscow are cleverer than you think. They may be a long way away, but they know everything there, let me tell you, *everything*!

They are all terrified.

MAYOR. Well, that's as may be, we shall soon find out; at least you've been warned. I've taken certain precautions myself, you'd best do the same, all of you. 'Specially you, Artemy Philipovich! (*To the* CHARITY COMMISSIONER.) This Inspector, he's sure to visit your hospital, you'd best see it's tidied up a bit. Give those patients of yours some clean night-caps, clean sheets, give them a good wash, last time I saw them they all looked like chimney sweeps!

CHARITY COMMISSIONER. We haven't got any sheets. . . .

MAYOR. Well, buy some, you've been charging for them for

twenty years, haven't you? [And label your patients, put a
notice over their beds in some foreign language – Latin, if
you can – with a list of dates and diseases, that sort of
thing.] And stop them smoking that foul tobacco, a civilized
man can't breathe in the place. You'd best throw half of
them out anyway, you've got far too many, the Inspector'll
think the doctor doesn't know his business.

CHARITY COMMISSIONER. He's a splendid doctor, [we've
got everything nicely organized.] Leave it to nature, that's
what we say. There's no point in spending a fortune on
expensive medicines. Man's a simple creature, if he's going
to get well, he'll get well and if he's going to die, then he'll
die. Anyway, the doctor's a German, he doesn't understand
a word anyone says.

DISTRICT PHYSICIAN (*beaming*). Ja. Onderstand everyt'ing!

MAYOR. Ha! And you, Amos Fyodorovich, you'd best do
something about that courthouse of yours, the place is like
a farmyard. Tell the porter to move his geese out of the
vestibule for a start, the petitioners have to sit there and
have their feet pecked at for hours on end. [Of course the
porter should be encouraged to keep poultry, but couldn't
you persuade him to keep them somewhere else? It's not
the thing in a magistrate's court, d'you see. I've been
meaning to speak to you about it for a long time.

JUDGE. Don't worry about that, I'll see he kills them today.
Perhaps you'd come to dinner tonight, Anton Antonovich?]

MAYOR (*ignoring the invitation*). Your courtroom, Amos
Fyodorovich, it's full of rubbish! All your hunting gear
lying about, riding crops in the dossier cupboard, boots up
on the bench, it's a terrible sight. I know you're fond of
hunting, but you clear all that away until this Inspector's
been and gone, you can put it all back later. And that clerk
of yours! Very clever man, I daresay, but he stinks of
vodka day and night! [It's not the thing for an officer of the
law. That's another thing I've been wanting to speak to you
about, only I keep forgetting. He ought to do something
about it, eat garlic or onions or get Doctor Christian to
give him some medicine.

DISTRICT PHYSICIAN. Ja, garlick. Gut! (*He beams.*)|

JUDGE. He says it's his natural smell. [He says his nurse dropped him when he was a baby, and he's smelt of vodka ever since.]

MAYOR. Well, [if it can't be helped, it can't.] I just thought I'd mention it, that's all. As for what Chmikhov calls 'our little weaknesses', that's not for me to talk about. No man is without sin, because that's the way the good Lord made us. [Voltaire can say what he likes, but he's a sinner just the same.

JUDGE. Depends what you mean by 'sin', Anton Antonovich.] There are sins and sins. I don't mind admitting I take bribes – but only thoroughbred puppies, you can't call that a sin.

MAYOR. Thoroughbred puppies are still bribes.

JUDGE. But not sinful bribes, Anton, there's the difference. Now if a man accepts a fur coat worth five hundred roubles, or a shawl for his wife . . .

MAYOR (*quickly*). That's no worse than accepting thoroughbred puppies, a bribe's a bribe. What's more, Anton, you don't believe in God. You never go to church! I am firm in my faith, at least. But you, when you go on about the Creation and all that, you make my hair stand on end!

JUDGE. I'm entitled to my opinions. I can think for myself!

MAYOR. That's dangerous, [too much thinking can be worse than none at all. Anyway, I only mentioned your courthouse in passing, nobody'd be such a fool as to want to go in there, it ought to have fallen down long ago. It must be under divine protection.] And you, Luka Lukich – your teachers! [You're the Schools Superintendent,] you ought to have done something about them long ago. I know they're clever men, educated and that, but they seem a funny lot to me. There's that one – you know, whatsisname, the one with the twisted nose – can't stand up in front of class without pulling the most terrible faces. [Like this, d'you see. (*He pulls a face.*)] Now that's all right, pulling faces to the boys, that's all part of their education, I suppose, but what happens if he pulls them at the Inspector?

SCHOOLS SUPERINTENDENT. [But what can I do? I've told him but he takes no notice. The other day, when Prince Miloffsky called in to look round the school, he was pulling such scarey faces the Prince accused me of letting the boys be taught by a free-thinker!

MAYOR. That's terrible, terrible! And what about that History master? Very clever, very brainy, knows his subject inside out, I'm sure, but why does he have to get so excited? He's all right on the Assyrians and the Babylonians, but I heard him once on Alexander the Great and I thought the school was on fire, the way he carried on. He jumped out of his desk, snatched up his chair and smashed it to the ground. I know Alexander was a hero, but that's no excuse for breaking up Government property, is it?]

SCHOOLS SUPERINTENDENT. It's just his enthusiasm. I've told him about it several times, but he always says, 'I would lay down my life in the cause of learning.' . . . You can't say much to that, can you?

MAYOR. That's a funny thing about life – all the cleverest men are mad. Mad! They either drink themselves to death, or pull faces that would shame the devil.

SCHOOLS SUPERINTENDENT (*gloomily*). I wouldn't want my worst enemy to work in education. Everyone's afraid of everyone else, everyone interferes with you, everyone wants to prove he's cleverer than you are. It's a dog's life.

MAYOR. It wouldn't matter, all that, if it wasn't for this damned Inspector, this in-cog-nit-o! Any moment he could come bursting in through that door (*He points.*), looking for you. 'Ah, here you all are,' he'll say. 'Where's that Judge? – Lyapkin-Tyapkin – hand him over. And who's the Charity Commissioner? – Zlemyanika. Let me have him . . . District Physician? – Doctor Christian – come with me!' It's terrifying, terrifying!

THE DISTRICT PHYSICIAN *laughs his head off.*
Enter the POSTMASTER. *They all jump with fear.*

POSTMASTER. What's all this I hear about a Government Inspector?

MAYOR. When did you hear?

POSTMASTER. Just now. Peter Ivanovich Bobchinsky came into the Post Office to tell me.

MAYOR. What do you make of it, then?

POSTMASTER. It's obvious.

MAYOR. What's obvious?

POSTMASTER. There's going to be a war with the Turks.

JUDGE. Just what I said!

MAYOR. Nonsense!

POSTMASTER. It'll be war with the Turks, you'll see. Those damned French are behind it, as usual, they'll never learn. Well, they'll get more than they bargained for this time!

MAYOR. Stop being an idiot, Ivan Kuzmich! We're the one's who'll get more than we bargained for, not the Turks. (*He hands the* POSTMASTER *his letter.*) Read this!

POSTMASTER. Aha, a letter! That's different. Perhaps it won't be war with the Turks, after all.

MAYOR. *Read!* (*Pause.*) Well?

POSTMASTER. Well, what?

MAYOR. What about it? How do you feel about it?

POSTMASTER. What about you? How do you feel about it?

MAYOR. Me? [Oh, it's nothing to me,] I'm not worried. Well, of course, there's the shopkeepers, a few tradesmen, I know, I know, they're always complaining about me, but as God's my judge, if I ever accepted a penny from anybody it was all done without a scrap of ill-feeling on either side . . . (*He takes the* POSTMASTER'*s arm and leads him downstage.*) D'you think someone could have sent in a – a secret report about me? Whyever else should they send an Inspector down here? Listen, Ivan Kuzmich, don't you think that – for all our sakes – you could just take a peek at all the letters that come through your Post Office? You know, unseal them, quick look, seal them up, no harm done? [Then if there's nothing nasty there, no denunciation or anything, you just send them on.]

POSTMASTER. Actually, I always do, Anton Antonovich. I do it more out of curiosity than as a precaution, though. Some people's letters are so interesting – [you'd be amazed what you can learn,] it's better than the newspapers.

MAYOR. [Anything's better than the newspapers.] But you haven't come across anything about this official from Petersburg?

POSTMASTER. Not from Petersburg, no, but [there's been plenty about officials in Saratov and Kostroma – really juicy stuff, some of it, it's a pity you never saw any of it. And] there was this letter from a lieutenant to his friend, describing some dance he'd been to – very daring, some of it. 'My life is spent in the Elysian fields,' he wrote, yes, yes! 'With orchestras playing, and flags flying, and hordes of beautiful women longing to be my slaves . . .' yes, yes. Oh, there was so much *feeling* in that letter, Anton Antonovich! I had to keep it, I liked it so much. (*He produces the letter.*) Shall I read it to you?

MAYOR. Not now; some other time. But you'll do me that little favour, won't you, Ivan Kuzmich – unseal 'em, quick look, seal 'em up again. Anything compromising, don't hesitate, do your duty, keep it back.

POSTMASTER. Certainly, with pleasure, Anton Antonovich.

JUDGE (*overhearing the last exchange*). You'll find yourselves in trouble, you two, if you're not careful. [One little slip, Ivan Kuzmich, and you'll find yourself reduced to Civil Officer, Seventh Class.] Remember, it only took one spark to set Moscow on fire.

MAYOR. Oh, nonsense! We're not going to make public use of the letters. [It's just a little arrangement between friends.

JUDGE. Mind you, I think you're right, there's trouble in the wind, I can always smell it coming. (*He brings the* MAYOR *downstage.*) By the way, Anton Antonovich, old friend, I've been meaning to give you a little present, only I keep forgetting. A bitch puppy it is, sister to that splendid hound of mine. Of course as far as shooting's concerned, I'm really in clover now. You know Tcheptovich is suing Varhovinsky? Ha! So I get free shooting on both their estates. I could take you along. . . .

MAYOR (*breaking away from him*). Good God, who cares about your free shooting, today of all days.] I can't get this damned in-cog-nit-o out of my head! I'm sure that any moment that door's going to open and ...

The door bursts open and in come BOBCHINSKY *and* DOBCHINSKY, *out of breath.*

BOBCHINSKY. Something quite extraordinary has happened!

DOBCHINSKY. Something really unexpected!

ALL. What?
What is it?
What's happened?

DOBCHINSKY. You'll never credit it. We went down to the inn ...

BOBCHINSKY. Yes, I was going to the inn with Peter Ivanovich ...

DOBCHINSKY. Please, Peter Ivanovich, I'm telling it!

BOBCHINSKY. No, no! Please! Let me, let me! You'll never get it right, let me tell it!

DOBCHINSKY. You'll muddle it all up and forget the best bits, I know you will!

BOBCHINSKY. I won't, I won't, I'm sure I won't! Don't interrupt, now, let me tell the story and don't interrupt! Gentlemen, please, tell Peter Ivanovich not to interrupt!

MAYOR. Heavens above, stop squabbling and speak, for the love of God! [You've got our hearts in our boots, sit down and put us out of our misery, one of you!] Here, Peter Ivanovich, here's a chair for you ... and one for you, Peter Ivanovich.

They all seat themselves around the two PETER IVANOVICHES.

Now then, what's all this about?

BOBCHINSKY (*to* DOBCHINSKY). Allow me, please! (*He collects himself.*) W-e-e-e-ll ... I'll begin at the beginning. (*To the* MAYOR.) As soon as I had the pleasure of leaving you, after you'd had that upsetting letter, [I ran off,] do you see – [Oh, please, Peter Ivanovich, don't interrupt, I know all of it, all of it! Well, do you see,] I dashed in to see Korobkin, but Korobkin wasn't at home, so I ran on to Rastakovsky's but Rastakovsky wasn't at home either, so then I popped in to see Ivan Kuzmich here – (*He indicates the* POSTMASTER.) – and he *was* at home, so I gave him the news about this Government Inspector. W-e-e-e-ll, coming away from Ivan Kuzmich I happened to run into Peter Ivanovich . . .

DOBCHINSKY. Near the stall where they sell hot pies.

BOBCHINSKY. Near the stall where they sell hot pies. I met Peter Ivanovich and I said to him: Have you heard the news Anton Antonovich had in his letter? But Peter Ivanovich had already heard all about it from your house-keeper – (*To the* MAYOR.) – Avdotya, who'd been on some errand to Phillip Antonovich Pochechuev, I can't remember what . . .

DOBCHINSKY. To fetch a keg of French brandy.

BOBCHINSKY. To fetch a keg of French brandy. So we went off – Peter Ivanovich and I went off – to see Pochechuev –

DOBCHINSKY. And I said –

BOBCHINSKY. Now, please, Peter Ivanovich, don't interrupt, you mustn't interrupt – we were on our way to see Pochechuev when Peter Ivanovich said to me, 'Let's go into the inn,' he said, 'I've had nothing to eat all day and my stomach's beginning to rumble' – Peter Ivanovich's stomach, that is, do you see – 'let's go into the inn,' he kept saying, 'they've got some fresh salmon in and we could just have a little bite.' S-o-o-o . . . we'd no sooner got into the inn than this young man . . .

DOBCHINSKY. Quite well dressed, but not in uniform . . .

BOBCHINSKY. Quite well dressed, but not in uniform . . . came in and strolled across the room with such a thoughtful expression, do you know, very serious . . . nice manners . . . gestures . . . and a look, do you know, as if he'd got a lot (*He taps his forehead.*) – up *here*! And suddenly I had a kind of presentiment, and I said to Peter Ivanovich here, I said, 'There's more in this than meets the eye,' I said. Yes! Well, Peter Ivanovich called over the innkeeper, you know, Vlass – his wife had a son three weeks ago, such a bright little chap he is, he'll be running an inn like his father one day, you'll see. . . . So Peter Ivanovich asks this Vlass, quietly, do you see, 'Who is that young man?' he asks, and this Vlass says, 'That young man,' he says . . .

DOBCHINSKY. . . . Is an offic –

BOBCHINSKY. Oh, please don't interrupt, Peter Ivanovich, you couldn't possibly tell the story properly, [you've got a lithp,] ever since you lost that tooth you've talked with a whistle. . . . 'That young man,' says Vlass, 'is an *official*, from Petersburg he is, and his name,' says Vlass, 'is Ivan Alexandrovich Khlyestakov, and he's on his way,' says Vlass, 'to Saratov, so he says, and his behaviour,' says Vlass, 'is very peculiar, very peculiar indeed,' says Vlass, 'he's been here nearly two weeks, he's had everything on credit, he hasn't parted with a penny since he arrived and he shows no signs of wanting to leave!' – says Vlass. And it was as he was saying that, that suddenly it dawned on me, and I said to Peter Ivanovich, 'Aha!' I said . . .

DOBCHINSKY. No, Peter Ivanovich, it was me that said 'Aha!' first!

BOBCHINSKY. All right, you said it first, but then I said it. 'Aha' I said . . .

DOBCHINSKY. So did I.

BOBCHINSKY. ⎫
DOBCHINSKY. ⎬ Aha!

BOBCHINSKY (*furious*) . . . we *both* said, 'If he's really going to Saratov,' we said, 'why is he staying here?' we said. '*This*,' we said, 'must be,' we said, 'the *one*!'

MAYOR. The what?

BOBCHINSKY. The official.

MAYOR. What official?

BOBCHINSKY. The official you were warned about in that letter, Anton Antonovich! The Government Inspector!

MAYOR. Dear God, no! Never. It can't be!

DOBCHINSKY. It must be. He doesn't pay his bills, and he doesn't go on with his journey, do you see! Who else could he be?

BOBCHINSKY. It *is* him, it *is*, I swear it! You should have seen how he watched us, how he examined everything! He saw that we were eating salmon – for Peter Ivanovich's stomach, do you see – and he came right across and just stood there, staring down at our plates. It gave me quite a turn.

MAYOR (*closing his eyes*). Lord, have mercy on us sinners! (*To* BOBCHINSKY.) Which room is he in? Did you find out?

DOBCHINSKY. Number five. The one under the stairs.

BOBCHINSKY. Where the officers had that fight last year.

MAYOR. Did you find out how long he's been here?

DOBCHINSKY. A fortnight. He arrived on St Basil's Day.

MAYOR. Mother of God protect us! A fortnight! In the last fortnight the Sergeant's widow's been flogged, the convicts haven't been fed, the streets haven't been swept, the whole town's like a cess-pit! [Oh, the disgrace! The ignominy!] (*He clutches his head.*)

CHARITY COMMISSIONER. Well, Anton Antonovich, what are we going to do? Shall we all go along to the Inn . . . ?

JUDGE. No, no, let the priests and the tradesmen go along first, that's the proper thing. A good reputation stands still, it's the bad ones that run like the wind.

MAYOR. Reputation be damned. Let me handle this my way, please. It's a stupid mouse that only knows one hole. [We've been in some tough spots in the past, and I've always got us out of them – and been praised for it afterwards, too! With God's help we'll get out of this one as well. (*To* BOBCHINSKY.) You say he's a young man?

BOBCHINSKY. Young, yes. Under thirty, I'd swear.

MAYOR. All the better. Young men are easier to deal with, there's always a chink in their armour.] Now, gentlemen, off you go, you've all got muck in your own backyards. I shall take Dobchinsky round to the Inn – just a casual visit, you know, just dropping in to make sure the visitors are being looked after properly, the way I always do. Svistunov!

SVISTUNOV (*rushing forward*). Sir?

MAYOR. Run and fetch the Superintendent, as quick as you can. No, no, don't go, I shall need you here, go and tell someone else to fetch the Superintendent, and then you come back here.

    SVISTUNOV *runs off.*

CHARITY COMMISSIONER (*to the* JUDGE). Come on, we best be away, this looks like real trouble.

JUDGE. [I don't know what you've got to worry about, Artemy Philipovich. All you've got to do is hand out a few clean nightgowns and you're in the clear.

CHARITY COMMISSIONER. Clean nightgowns! I'm not worried about nightgowns. There's some stupid regulation says the patients have got to have beef tea every day, but the whole place stinks of cabbage soup, you can't go in there without holding your nose.]

JUDGE. Well, I refuse to get worked up. Who on earth would want to inspect a district courthouse, anyway? [God help anyone who tried to make head or tail of all those books and papers, he'd curse the day he was born.] I've been on the bench here for fifteen years, and I've never yet seen a single report I could understand. Solomon himself couldn't tell right from wrong in this place. . . .

The JUDGE, *the* CHARITY COMMISSIONER, *the* SCHOOLS SUPERINTENDENT *and the* POSTMASTER *go out, colliding in the doorway with* CONSTABLE SVISTUNOV, *who is returning.*

MAYOR (*to* SVISTUNOV). Well, is the carriage ready?

SVISTUNOV. All ready, Your Honour.

MAYOR. Right, go out and . . . no, stop, don't. Wait! Go and fetch me . . . where the devil have all the police got to? Where's Prohorov, he was told to be here.

SVISTUNOV. He's at the station, Your Honour, but he can't go on duty.

MAYOR. Can't? What d'you mean, can't?

SVISTUNOV. He was brought in dead drunk this morning, Your Honour. We put two buckets o' water on'm, Your Honour, but a' won't stand up yet.

MAYOR (*clutching his hair*). Mother of God, what next? Go on out, Constable, quick! . . . no, stop, run to my room first, d'you hear, and fetch me my sword and my new hat. Quick, quick, quick! (*To* DOBCHINSKY.) Come on, Dobchinsky, let's go, then.

BOBCHINSKY. Me too, me too, oh, please, Anton Antonovich, let me come too!

MAYOR. No, no, I'm sorry, Bobchinsky, you can't, you really

can't. [It would be too awkward, d'you see, and] anyway there'd be no room in the carriage.

BOBCHINSKY. I don't mind that, [I'll manage somehow.] I'll run along behind, [I won't try to get in!] I only want to peep through the crack in the door, just to see what happens. . . .

SVISTUNOV *enters with the sword and a hatbox.*

MAYOR. Here, hold this, Dobchinsky. (*He hands the hatbox to* DOBCHINSKY.) And you hold this, Bobchinsky. (*He hands the hat to* BOBCHINSKY.) (*The* MAYOR *then turns to* SVISTUNOV.) Now run along, fetch the rest of the police, tell them to . . . look at that, I ask you, just look at that blade, all chipped and scratched. Is that a fit sword for a Mayor to carry around? Of course it never occurs to anyone to send me a new one! What a bunch of crooks – I bet they're cooking up a pack of lies about me this very minute! (*Turning to* SVISTUNOV *again.*) [Go and round up the rest of the police, tell them they're each to take a street in their hands . . . what the devil am I saying! – take a broom in their hands and start sweeping the streets – tell them to start near the hotel. And tell them they best sweep it clean – the street, I mean, not the hotel.] And you watch out – yes, you! Oh, I'm on to you, make no mistake! [I know the way my silver spoons have got into the habit of slipping into your bootlegs. You best watch it, my boy!] I'm not as blind as you think I am! What's your game with Schernayev, the draper, eh? Eh? He offers you a couple of yards of broadcloth and what do you do, eh? Walk off with the whole roll, don't you, eh? You best be a bit careful, lad, you're taking more than you're entitled to, you're not a sergeant yet. (*He pushes* SVISTUNOV.) Go, on, off with you.

As SVISTUNOV *goes off the* POLICE INSPECTOR *enters.* Ah, Stefan Ilyich, there you, are, where the devil have you been? You want to disgrace me, do you?

POLICE INSPECTOR. I've been out by the gate all the time.

MAYOR. [Nonsense.] Do you realize this Government Inspector is in the town already? What have you done about it, eh?

POLICE INSPECTOR. [What you said. Pugovitzin's taking all my men out to sweep the streets.]

MAYOR. Where's Dyerzhimorda?

POLICE INSPECTOR. Gone to see if the fire-engine's working.

MAYOR. Good. And Prohorov? I'm told he's drunk.

POLICE INSPECTOR. He's out cold. You can't make an empty sack stand up.

MAYOR [How d'you let that happen, then?

POLICE INSPECTOR. There was a fight on the outskirts yesterday and I sent Prohorov to settle it. He came back absolutely stoned, I don't know why.]

MAYOR. Savages! Now listen to me. Station Pugovitzin on the bridge, he'll look very impressive there, he's tall. Get some of the others to pull down that rotten fence by the cobbler's and stick up a few police notices as if there was some public building going on. No, stop! [Dear God,] I forgot all about the pile of stinking rubbish behind that fence, [forty carts wouldn't shift that lot in a week!] God, what a cess-pit this town is! [Put up a fence, a monument, anything, anywhere, and before you can turn round it's been smothered in rubbish, the devil knows where it all comes from. (*He sighs.*) Now then, another thing, if this damned Inspector comes nosing around any of your men, asking them if they're happy in their work, they're to say, straight out: 'Yes, Your Honour, perfectly happy.' D'you see. And if any of them aren't happy, I'll give them something to be unhappy about, afterwards, just you tell them that, Stefan Ilyich.] Ah me, I'm a sinful man! (*He picks up the hatbox.*) If God sees we get through all this, I'll light Him the biggest candle He's ever seen! I'll make every rotten tradesman in the town give me a hundredweight of wax for that candle, [you wait and see!] (*He prays.*) Dear God, protect us! (*To* DOBCHINSKY.) Come on, Dobchinsky, let's go!

He puts the box on his head.

POLICE INSPECTOR. That's a hatbox, Anton Antonovich, not a hat.

MAYOR (*flinging the box down*). I can see that, you fool!

Listen, [I've thought of something else!] If this Inspector asks about the chapel for the hospital – you know, the one we got a grant for five years past – don't forget, it burnt down. I sent in a report about it. Some idiot's bound to forget and say it was never started, I just know they will. And tell Constable Dyerzhimorda to keep his fists to himself – he seems to think the best way to keep order is to give everyone a black eye, as a matter of principle. (*He starts to go, then runs back.*) And don't let the soldiers out in the street half naked! Every time I go near the barracks, there they are, walking about in nothing but their shirts, it's a scandal – why can't they be issued with trousers?

He rushes out, followed by the others. Enter the MAYOR'S WIFE *and their daughter*, MARIA.

ANNA (*off*). Where are they? Dear God, where's everyone gone? (*Coming through the door.*) Anton! Antosha! Toni! Where are you? (*To* MARIA, *very fast.*) It's all your fault, girl, you and your fussing. 'Wait while I pin this, wait while I tie that . . .!' (*She runs to the window, leans out and calls.*) Toni! Where are you off to? What's happening? Is it the Inspector? Has he got a moustache? What sort of moustache has he got? What?

MAYOR (*off*). Later, my dear, later.

ANNA. Later, what does he mean, later? What's the use of later? (*Shouting.*) Tell me his rank at least, Antosha! Is he a colonel? (*She gives up. To* MARIA.) There, he's gone! I'll make him pay for that! And as for you! (*Mimicking.*) 'Oh, Mamma, Mamma, wait for me, Mamma, help me fasten my collar, Mamma . . .' And now see what happens, we know nothing, nothing! You and your vanity! Just because the Postmaster is here you go prinking and preening over the mirror. You think he's sweet on you, but the moment your back's turned he doesn't even know you exist, so!

MARIA. [Never mind, Mamma, it can't be helped now.] We'll know all about it in an hour or two.

ANNA. Oh, thank you very much, that's lovely! Why stop at an hour, though, why not a month or two while you're at it?

(*She leans out of the window.*) Hey, Avdotya, have you heard anything, eh ? Has anyone arrived ?

AVDOTYA (*off*). He just waved me aside!

ANNA. Dear God, what a fool that girl is! What d'you mean, waved you aside, you shouldn't have let him wave you aside, you could have jumped in front of him, couldn't you ? Idiot, you're as bad as Maria, all you two think of is young men, I know!

AVDOTYA (*off*). They were too quick!

ANNA. What ? They were too quick! Well, you be quick too, go on, run after them, find out where they've gone, and find out about this stranger, I want to know everything, everything, d'you hear ? Look through the keyhole if you have to, see what colour his eyes are, what sort of moustache he's got, whether he's handsome or not . . . and mind you come straight back! Go on, don't just stand there, hurry, hurry, hurry. . . .

She is still shouting as the curtain falls.

SCENE TWO

A small room at the hotel; bed, table, chair, trunk, empty bottle, top-boots, clothes brush. OSSIP *lounges on the bed with his boots on.*

OSSIP. Gawd, I'm so hungry! I'm so empty I reckon my belly must think my throat's been cut! We don't look no nearer getting home, neither. I dunno. It must be nigh on two months since we left Petersburg. His lordship's been chucking his money about all over the place, and now all we can do is hide away here [with our tails between our legs] and hope for a bloomin' miracle. There'd have been plenty for the whole journey if he didn't have to be so grand every place we stop for the night. (*He mimics* KHLYESTA-KOV.) 'Ai say, Ossip, old chap, cut along and book me the best room in the place, will you ? Oh, and order me a decent meal, the very best they've got. Ai simply can't stomach inferior food!' As if he really was somebody! Instead of just a stuck-up little clerk, one cut above an office boy! That's all he is! But he'll put on airs with anybody; out come the cards, and he starts throwing his money away like a millionaire. So now here we are, cleaned out! I'm fed up with him!

Mind you, I'm not saying there's anything against living in the country – not much going on, but then there's less to worry about. [Find yourself a decent wench, you could lie about by the stove all day eating home-made pies, not a care in the world.] But it's not the life for me. Give me Petersburg, every time. You need a bit of the ready, of course, but it's a grand life – theatres, dance-halls, races, the lot! [You can sit next to the officials on the ferry or listen to the officers talking about army life, or what the stars foretell, and all that.] And the way they talk – they call you 'Sir' in the shops, not like here. Very classy in Petersburg. Then there's the women! Take a walk through any of the parks, you can take your pick. Ladies' maids! Parlourmaids! Nursemaids! Housemaids! Aaaaah! (*He smirks and shakes his head.*)

[Oh, it's all polish and politeness in Petersburg! Everyone treats you like a gent! You feel a bit tired and you hop in a cab, lean back, take your ease like a lord! And if you don't happen to feel like paying, you just hop off again – there's a back door to every house, you just nip in one way and out the other, easy. Ah, that's the life!]

Only trouble is, it's all up and down with his lordship. One minute you're stuffing yourself silly, the next you're bloody starving . . . like now. I don't know what to do with him. His old man sends him money enough, but soon as he gets it – whoosh! He's off on the spree again, driving about in cabs all day, showing himself off at the opera every night, and inside a week he's floggin' his clothes again. And he'll let things go for next to nothing – a jacket worth a hundred and fifty – finest English cloth, the latest cut – he'll take a mouldy twenty-five for it. And trousers – he practically gives his trousers away! He'll go on till he hasn't got a shirt to his back; I've seen 'im walking about naked under his overcoat, it's terrible.

If only he'd get down to his job! He never goes near the office! He'd rather swank up and down the Nevsky or lose all his money at cards. If only the old master knew! (*To an imaginary Khlyestakov.*) Civil Servant or no Civil Servant, he'd up with your coat-tails and give you such a hiding you wouldn't sit down for a week. What I say is, if you've got a job to do, do it, and no mucking about.

Gawd, I'm so hungry I could eat a salt mine. And the landlord says no more grub till we've paid for what we've had – that means no more grub. I'd give my eye-teeth for a bowl of cabbage soup . . . aye, aye, somebody coming, sounds like his lordship. . . .

He jumps off the bed.

Enter KHLYESTAKOV.

KHLYESTAKOV. Here, take these. (*He hands* OSSIP *his hat and cane.*) You've been lounging on my bed again.

OSSIP. Lounging on your bed! What you mean? You think I've never seen a bed before?

KHLYESTAKOV. You've been lounging on it, you liar. Look, it's all mussed up!

OSSIP. What would I want with your rotten bed? I've got legs, I can stand, can't I? What do I want a bed for?

KHLYESTAKOV (*pacing up and down*). See if there's any tobacco left in the packet.

OSSIP. Ho, very likely! You know you smoked the last scrap four days ago . . . and that was dust.

KHLYESTAKOV (*pacing, twisting his mouth in different ways, then speaking, loud and determined*). Now, listen to me, Ossip . . .

OSSIP. Well, what?

KHLYESTAKOV (*still loud, but less assured*). You go down . . .

OSSIP. Down? Down where?

KHLYESTAKOV (*almost pleading*). Down to the dining room . . . Tell them . . . ask them . . . to send me up some lunch!

OSSIP. Not likely.

KHLYESTAKOV. What!

OSSIP. I don't feel like it.

KHLYESTAKOV. How dare you!

OSSIP. It's a waste of time, they won't send anything. The landlord said we'll get no more to eat until we pay the bill.

KHLYESTAKOV. What a nerve! The impudence of it!

OSSIP. He says he's going to the Mayor about it. 'You've been here over two weeks,' he says, 'and I haven't seen the colour of your money yet,' he says, 'you're nothing but a couple of common crooks,' he says – straight out.

KHLYESTAKOV. And what a kick you get out of repeating it, don't you?

OSSIP. 'If everyone was like you,' he says, 'the place'd be full of people living at my expense,' he says. 'I'm having no more mucking about,' he says, 'I'm going straight to the Mayor and have you two put in jail.'

KHLYESTAKOV. Shut up, you fool! [That's enough, now!] Get off down those stairs and tell them to send me up some lunch at once. Go on, move!

OSSIP (*gloomily*). I better tell the landlord to come and see you hisself.

KHLYESTAKOV. I don't want the landlord, I want the lunch! Go and tell him that!

OSSIP. But he won't . . .

KHLYESTAKOV (*wildly*). Oh, go on, get out! Bring the landlord if you want to, bring anyone you like, damn you!

He pushes OSSIP *out.*

It's a terrible thing, being as hungry as this. I thought a bit of a walk would help, but it's just made me hungrier than ever. If only I hadn't had such a good time at Penza, we'd still have some money to get home on. It was that infantry captain who finished me off. Had this amazing gift for dealing himself the ace! He can't have sat down with us for more than fifteen minutes, but he picked me clean as a bone! Wonderful! I'd like to have another go at that fellow sometime. There won't be anyone like him in this filthy little dump, that's certain. . . . They won't even give you a cabbage on tick, I've never met such a miserly bunch! *He walks up and down whistling. Enter* OSSIP *and the* WAITER.

WAITER. The landlord sent me to see what you want, sir.

KHLYESTAKOV. Ah! Good! Well, my dear chap, how are you, eh?

WAITER. Thank you, sir, I'm very well, sir, thanks be to God.

KHLYESTAKOV. Good, good! And how's business, eh? Everything flourishing?

WAITER. Oh, yes, sir, very busy, thanks be to God.

KHLYESTAKOV. Busy, eh? Plenty of visitors?

WAITER. Plenty enough, sir, thank you . . . and . . . er . . .

KHLYESTAKOV. And thank God, eh? Good, good. Well, now, old chap, they seem to have forgotten about my lunch down in the kitchen, and I've got an appointment this afternoon, so if you'd just nip down and hurry them up a bit. . . .

WAITER. I'm sorry, sir, but the landlord says as we're not to serve you no more. He says as he's going to complain to the Mayor about you, sir.

KHLYESTAKOV. Complain! What's he got to complain about? I'm the one to complain, not him! I've got to eat, haven't I? Everyone's got to eat! I shall waste away to nothing if I don't eat.

WAITER. I know, sir. Only the landlord says, 'I'm not giving him another crust till he's paid for what he's already 'ad.' His very own words, sir.

KHLYESTAKOV. But can't you tell him . . . explain to him . . . I mean, make him see reason . . . ?

WAITER. What can I say, sir?

KHLYESTAKOV. Tell him I've got to eat, of course! It's serious, he can't just let me starve! Money – what's money? You can't eat money, he'll get his money tomorrow, next week, sometime. It's all right for him, he's just a filthy peasant, he's probably used to going without, but he can't let a civilized man like me go hungry, it's ridiculous!

WAITER. I'll tell him what you say, sir.

The WAITER *and* OSSIP *go out.*

KHLYESTAKOV (*pacing*). What am I going to do if he still refuses? I've never been so hungry in my life! I suppose I could sell some clothes . . . my trousers . . . ? No, no, I mustn't, it's better to starve, I simply must arrive home in my Petersburg suit. It's a pity Ossip stopped me hiring that carriage, it would have been great turning up at home in my own carriage, dashing over to see a neighbour with all the lamps shining and Ossip perched up behind in some sort of livery, just like a real footman. (*Drawing himself up, playing the footman.*) 'Ivan Alexandrovich Khlyestakov, from Petersburg, is making his calls. Is the family in residence, my good fellow?' Bah! They wouldn't even know what 'in residence' means, the peasants. They're so crude they just push straight into a drawing room like a pack of bears. But I, I would drift elegantly over to the prettiest daughter . . . (*In foul French.*) 'Mademoiselle, enchanté . . .' (*He bows and scrapes.*) 'Mais vous sommes si beaux . . .' (*He grimaces.*) God, I'm so hungry I feel sick!

> *He holds his stomach.*
> *Enter* OSSIP.

Well?

OSSIP. They're sending up some lunch.

KHLYESTAKOV (*clapping and bouncing*). Dear God, how marvellous, lunch, lunch!

WAITER (*entering with a loaded tray*). Landlord says that's the very last time, now.

KHLYESTAKOV. 'Landlord says!!' Who cares about the rotten landlord! What have you brought?

WAITER. There's some soup, and a roast.

KHLYESTAKOV. What? Only two courses?

WAITER. That's all there is, sir.

KHLYESTAKOV. That's absurd, I'm not putting up with that! Go and tell him it's not enough.

WAITER. Landlord says it's too much, sir.

KHLYESTAKOV. And where's the gravy?

WAITER. There isn't any gravy, sir.

KHLYESTAKOV. Well, why not, eh? Tell me why not? I saw gravy with my own eyes this morning when I was passing the kitchen. And a lot of other things. There were two horrid little men in the dining room stuffing themselves with fresh salmon. Isn't there any of that left?

WAITER. Well, there is, sir, and then again, there isn't.

KHLYESTAKOV. What do you mean, 'Is, isn't'?

WAITER. In a manner of speaking, sir.

KHLYESTAKOV. No salmon?

WAITER. Only for the best customers, sir.

KHLYESTAKOV. Oh, you fool!

WAITER. Yes, sir.

KHLYESTAKOV. You're no better than a pig!

WAITER. No sir.

KHLYESTAKOV. Why should there be salmon for them and not for me, eh? Why? What's the difference between one traveller and another, eh?

WAITER. There is a difference, sir.

KHLYESTAKOV. Well? What is it?

WAITER. Some of them pays their bills, sir.

KHLYESTAKOV. Nonsense! I can't argue with an idiot! (*He ladles out some soup and eats greedily.*) What's this? You call this soup? They've just poured hot water into a dirty pot! It's got no taste at all! It just stinks of greasy dishes! I can't eat this, go and get something different.

WAITER. I'll take it away then, sir. Landlord said if you didn't like it you needn't have it.

KHLYESTAKOV (*protecting the food with his arms*). Leave it, leave it, you fool! You may be in the habit of treating your guests like this, but let me tell you I'm not in the habit of putting up with it! (*He drinks some soup.*) My God, what a foul brew! (*He goes on drinking.*) I can't believe anyone alive has ever tasted worse! Look, there's feathers floating in it! Whoever heard of feather soup? Here, Ossip, there's a bit of soup left if you want it. (*He tackles the roast.*) Good God, what on earth's this? It can't be meat!

WAITER. What is it, then?

KHLYESTAKOV. God alone knows, but it isn't meat, it's absolutely solid! They must have cooked the chopper by mistake. (*He tears at the meat.*) Oh, the crooks! Fancy giving people rubbish like this, it's enough to give you lockjaw. (*He is chewing madly.*) It's criminal! Look, it's like the bark of a tree! Ugh! (*He picks his teeth.*) Like splinters, won't come out! Filthy stuff, it'll probably turn my teeth black as coal! (*He wipes his mouth.*) Well, what else is there?

WAITER. Nothing, sir.

KHLYESTAKOV. Nothing! Oh, the brigands! No, gravy, no pudding, what do these scum think they're up to? They make me pay through the nose for a scrap of roast wood and some hot dishwater! It's disgusting. I shall complain to the Mayor!

> OSSIP *and the* WAITER *have hurriedly cleared the plates and left.*

It's just as if I'd eaten nothing at all! I've just whetted my appetite. If I had a penny to my name I'd send Ossip out for a bun.

> *Enter* OSSIP.

OSSIP. Here – the Mayor's downstairs . . . asking all sorts of questions about you.

KHLYESTAKOV (*terrified*). What? No! That damned landlord's complained already! Suppose he's come to take me to prison . . . ? Well, what of it, they'd have to treat me like a gentleman, and at least there'd be food. . . . No! No! I won't go, someone might see me, one of those officers or that pretty little daughter of the seed-merchant I've been flirting with, I can't let them all see me being dragged off to prison. Who the devil does he think he is, anyway, this landlord? I'm not some miserable shopkeeper or smelly labourer! (*Screwing up his courage.*) I'll tell him to his face. 'How dare you!' I'll say. 'Who do you think you are?' I'll say. 'Who the hell are you . . . ?'

> *The doorhandle turns, and* KHLYESTAKOV *grows pale and shrinks into himself. Enter the* MAYOR, *shutting the door on* DOBCHINSKY.
>
> KHLYESTAKOV *and the* MAYOR, *both equally terrified, stare at each other in silence for some moments. The* MAYOR *recovers first and comes to attention.*

MAYOR. May I take the liberty of wishing you good-day, sir?

KHLYESTAKOV (*bowing*). Much obleeged, I'm sure.

MAYOR. I hope you'll pardon the intrusion. . . .

KHLYESTAKOV. Not at all.

MAYOR. It's my duty, as senior official in the town, to see that all visitors and persons of rank and quality suffer no inconvenience. . . .

KHLYESTAKOV (*breaks in, stammering, but raising his voice as he goes on*). B-b-b-b-but what could I d-d-d-do . . . I'm g-g-going to p-p-pay, I really am, they're sending money from home . . .

    Enter DOBCHINSKY, *shutting the door on* BOBCHINSKY.
It's his fault, not mine. The food's uneatable, terrible, the meat's like shoe leather and the soup, God only knows what he puts in the soup. I had to throw some out the window just now. That man's starving me! And the tea . . . you'd never know it was tea, it stinks like fish-glue! Why should I . . . why . . . I don't see why . . .

MAYOR (*intimidated*). Please forgive me, it's really not my fault. The meat in the market's always good, I see to that, it's all brought in by good honest dealers, we've never had a complaint like this before. I really can't imagine where he could get bad meat. But sir, if you aren't satisfied with things here, I'd best escort you to other quarters. . . .

KHLYESTAKOV. No, no, no! I know what you mean with your 'other quarters' – you mean the jail. Well, I won't go! You've got no right, how dare you! I-I-I'm a Government official from Petersburg, I-I-I –

MAYOR (*aside*). Dear God, he's furious! Those damned shop-keepers have told him everything.

KHLYESTAKOV (*wildly bluffing*). You can bring a whole regi-ment with you, I still won't go! I'll write straight to the Minister, I will! (*He thumps the table.*) Who do you think you are? You . . . you . . . !

MAYOR (*trembling, stands to attention*). Oh, please, sir, have pity on us, don't ruin us! My wife . . . my little children . . . it'll ruin us!

KHLYESTAKOV. What's that got to do with it? Just because you've got a wife and children, you want me to go to jail?

BOBCHINSKY *peeps round the door, and withdraws in alarm.*

Well, I won't, so there!

MAYOR (*trembling*). It was my inexperience, sir, that's all. God knows it was all because of my inexperience, and because I'm paid so little, my official salary couldn't keep us in tea and sugar, I swear to God it couldn't. And if I've ever taken a bribe it's been nothing, nothing – something for the table, a little bit of cloth for a coat . . . trifles. And that story about me having the Sergeant's widow flogged, it's all lies, it's slander, sir, put about by my enemies! There's people here so jealous of my position they'd kill me if they dared!

KHLYESTAKOV. Well, it's nothing to do with me, all that. (*Thoughtfully.*) Why tell me all this – what do I care about your enemies, and some rotten Sergeant's rotten widow? You needn't think you can flog me, the way you did that poor woman. Oh, no, you've got a long way to go before you can do that, the idea of it! I'll pay my bill . . . I'll pay . . . I just don't happen to have any money at the moment, that's all . . . That's why I'm stuck in this ghastly place, I just haven't a penny to pay with.

MAYOR (*aside*). Ar, 'at's a crafty little fellow. That's a broad enough hint, but there's such a fog of words around it you can't be certain. Ah, well – what has to be, has to be. (*To* KHLYESTAKOV.) Sir, if you should happen to be temporarily short of – er – ready money, sir, or of anything else, sir, why, sir, it's my duty to help out visitors, so I'm at your service.

KHLYESTAKOV. Ready money . . . ! Yes, yes, could you, would you, lend me a little, just to pay off that damned landlord . . . a couple of hundred would do . . . possibly even . . . less . . . ?

MAYOR (*handing him a sheaf of notes*). Two hundred, of course. It's a pleasure, please don't bother to count them, it's exactly right.

KHLYESTAKOV (*taking the money*). Much obleeged, I'm sure. Of course, I'll send it straight back the moment I get to my estate, I never delay over things like that. I can see you're a real gentleman, sir, and I'm sorry if I misjudged you. Things will be quite different now. (*He calls.*) Hey, Ossip!

MAYOR (*aside*). He took it like a lamb, thank God. [Things ought to go a bit easier now.] I managed to slip him four hundred instead of two.

Enter OSSIP.

KHLYESTAKOV. Ossip, fetch that waiter back here. (OSSIP *goes off.*) (*To the* MAYOR *and* DOBCHINSKY.) But why are you both standing, gentlemen? Please sit down. (*To* DOBCHINSKY.) Sit down, sir, please.

MAYOR. It's all right, we don't mind standing.

KHLYESTAKOV. No, please, I won't have it, sit down, do! I see now what kind and generous people you are. I confess that at first I thought you'd come to . . . (*To* DOBCHINSKY.) Sit down!

They sit, uneasily. BOBCHINSKY *peeps through the door.*

MAYOR (*aside*). He wants to stay incognito, we'll have to go along with it. (*Aloud to* KHLYESTAKOV.) We just popped in – that is, Peter Ivanovich Dobchinsky here, [he's a local landowner,] and me – thought we'd pop in here and see how they're treating the visitors. . . . That's part of my duties, you know, I'm not the sort of Mayor who leaves everything to look after itself. I take my responsibilities as an official and a Christian seriously. My only reward is the occasional pleasure of meeting someone really distinguished, like yourself.

KHLYESTAKOV. The pleasure's mine, sir. If it hadn't been for you I might have been stuck in this dump for ages – I hadn't the faintest idea how I was going to pay the bill.

MAYOR (*aside*). Oh, yes, very likely! Couldn't pay his bill, indeed! (*Aloud to* KHLYESTAKOV.) And may I take the liberty, sir, of asking you where you might be travelling to?

KHLYESTAKOV. I'm off home, old chap. To my estate in Saratov.

MAYOR (*aside*). Saratov, he says – and without a blush, too! I'm going to have to watch this one. (*Aloud.*) Very nice too, a delightful journey. They say travel broadens the mind, though on some of these roads it isn't only the mind that gets broadened. . . . I take it you're travelling for pleasure, sir?

KHLYESTAKOV. No. My father sent for me. The old boy's all worked up because I haven't been promoted yet, he seems to think they start pinning decorations on you the moment you arrive in Petersburg! I'd like to see how he'd get on if he had to hang around my rotten office all day!

MAYOR (*aside*). Dragging in his old father now, that's a good one! (*Aloud.*) Will you be staying long on your estate, sir?

KHLYESTAKOV. I really can't say. My father's as stupid as a mule, and just as obstinate. He can say what he likes, I just *can't* live anywhere but Petersburg, and there's an end to it. 'I'm not going to waste my life among peasants,' I shall say, 'my soul is a-thirst for culture. The world has changed,' I shall tell him, 'since you were young!'

MAYOR (*aside*). At's a first class liar, no mistake – never dries up, never puts a foot wrong. [Looks as if you could knock him down with a feather, too.] I'll catch him out yet, though. (*Aloud.*) Of course, sir, you're absolutely right. What can anyone do out in the wilds, away from the people who matter. Take my case, now – I can be up all night, slaving away, trying to do my best for the country – but where's the recognition, eh? Who's to know about it? (*He looks round the room.*) This room looks damp to me.

KHLYESTAKOV. Damp? The place is a sewer! And you should see the bed-bugs – they bite like wolf-hounds.

MAYOR. Dear God, that's terrible! A distinguished visitor being exposed to that sort of thing, it's scandalous. Very likely the room's a bit dark for you, too, sir?

KHLYESTAKOV. Like the depths of hell. That damned land-lord won't even give me a candle to read by. Now and then one feels like a bit of culture – read an essay or two, scribble the odd poem, but one can't, it's too dark.

MAYOR. I wonder if I might . . . ? Oh, no, I can't. I'm unworthy!

KHLYESTAKOV. What? What is it?

MAYOR. No, really, I'm not worthy.

KHLYESTAKOV. Worthy of what, for heaven's sake?

MAYOR. [If only I dared,] I'd . . . I have this lovely room in my house, d'you see, quite empty . . . full of light . . . quite . . . if only I dared . . . but no, I can't. It would be too great an honour. Please pardon any presumption, it's only my simple nature that makes me want to offer . . .

KHLYESTAKOV. On the contrary, old chap, I'd be delighted, really! I'd much rather be in a private house than in this disgusting tavern.

MAYOR. And I shall be delighted! My wife will be delighted! My daughter will be delighted! I've always put hospitality first, ever since I was a child! Especially when my guest is a real personage like yourself. Oh, please, please don't think I'm flattering you, that's not my way at all. I speak straight from the heart.

KHLYESTAKOV. I'm much obleeged, old chap. I'm the same myself – I just can't stand hypocrites. I like your frankness and cordiality, they're the first things I look for in people. I confess I ask for nothing more in life than honesty and sympathy. Honesty and sympathy, that's all I ask.

Enter the WAITER *and* OSSIP; BOBCHINSKY *peeps round the door again.*

WAITER. You sent for me, sir.

KHLYESTAKOV. Yes, I want the bill.

WAITER. I gave it to you this morning, sir. Again.

KHLYESTAKOV. I don't keep your filthy bits of paper. How much was it?

WAITER. Well, now, you had full dinner the first night, smoked salmon for lunch next day – them you paid for. After that it was all on tick, so . . .

KHLYESTAKOV. Idiot! I don't want a list of what I had, I want to know how much I owe.

MAYOR. Please, sir, don't upset yourself, let it wait. (*To the* WAITER.) You can go. I'll see the bill's paid.

KHLYESTAKOV (*putting his money away*). Yes, of course, much better.

The WAITER *goes off.* BOBCHINSKY *peeps in.*

MAYOR. Would Your Honour perhaps care to look over some of our public buildings, I wonder?

KHLYESTAKOV. Whatever for?

MAYOR. Why, sir, to see how we do things here, how the town's administered, and so on and so forth.

KHLYESTAKOV. Well, all right, if you like.

BOBCHINSKY *peeps in again.*

MAYOR. You could have a look at the school, see how we teach the children. . . .

KHLYESTAKOV. Oh, certainly, certainly.

MAYOR. And then we could go down to the police station, visit the cells . . . ?

KHLYESTAKOV. Why the police station? . . . I'd much rather see the hospital.

MAYOR. Of course, Your Honour, of course, anything you say! Would you rather go in your carriage or will you do me the honour of sharing mine?

KHLYESTAKOV. I'll come with you, please.

MAYOR (*to* DOBCHINSKY). There won't be room for you.

DOBCHINSKY. It doesn't matter, I'll be all right.

MAYOR (*aside to* DOBCHINSKY). Listen, you've got to run like the wind, deliver a message to my wife. (*To* KHLYESTAKOV.) Will you excuse me, sir, if I just scribble a short note to my wife? She'll want to prepare for such a distinguished guest.

KHLYESTAKOV. Will she really? Well, there's ink here, but I don't think there's any paper. Here, what about this bill, will that do?

MAYOR. Splendid, splendid, thank you. (*He writes, muttering to himself.*) We'll see how things are after he's had a good lunch and a few bottles of wine – get out that local Madeira. It looks innocent enough but a couple of good glasses'd make an elephant stagger. If only I knew a bit more about him, I'd know what to watch out for. There, now hurry!

He hands the note to DOBCHINSKY, *who moves towards the door. At this moment the door comes off its hinges and* BOBCHINSKY *comes flying into the room on top of it. General exclamations of alarm.* BOBCHINSKY *scrambles up.*

KHLYESTAKOV. I say, have you hurt yourself?

BOBCHINSKY. Do, do, it's dothing, dothing at all, please don't bodder! I've just bruised the bridge of by dose, dat's all. I'll rud over to Doctor Christian's, he's got a barvellous plaster thing, he'll put it right id do tibe.

MAYOR (*furious with* BOBCHINSKY). It doesn't matter, it's nothing. Will it please Your Honour to come now? Your man can bring over your luggage. (*To* OSSIP.) Bring everything round to the Mayor's house, anyone will show you the way. (*He shows out* KHLYESTAKOV *formally*.) No, sir, after you, please! (*He follows, but turns back at the doorway*.) That's typical, typical! Couldn't you find someone else's door to knock down? [Coming tumbling into the room like a circus clown!] (*He takes a few more steps and turns*.) Bah! [Numbskull!]

> The MAYOR *stalks out*. BOBCHINSKY, *head hanging, slowly follows*.

CURTAIN

SCENE THREE

The MAYOR's *house.*
The MAYOR's *wife,* ANNA, *and his daughter,* MARIA, *are still standing by the window.*

ANNA. Oh, it's monstrous! Here we are, still hanging about with no idea what's going on, all because of your prinking and preening over the dressing table! I wish I'd never listened to you. Oh, isn't it infuriating! Not a soul in sight, it's just as if the whole town was dead! You'd think they were doing it on purpose!

MARIA. Really, Mamma, [we're sure to know all about it in a few minutes,] Avdotya can't possibly be much longer . . . (*Peering out of the window, she suddenly screams*.) Mamma, Mamma, look, someone's coming, look, right at the end of the street!

ANNA. Where? I can't see anyone. You're always imagining things, girl!

MARIA. There!

ANNA. Oh, yes, so there is! Who is it? It's a man . . . very small . . . dressed like a gentleman . . . oh, who can it be, how maddening, who on earth can it be?

MARIA. It's Dobchinsky, Mamma.

ANNA. Dobchinsky! Don't be ridiculous, you're imagining things again, it's no more Dobchinsky than . . . (*She leans out of the window, waving her handkerchief.*) Hey! You! Come here! Hurry!

MARIA. It really is Dobchinsky, Mamma.

ANNA. Don't contradict me, I tell you it's not.

MARIA. [There, now, look! Wasn't I right?] It's Dobchinsky.

ANNA. Of course it's Dobchinsky, I can see that for myself, what are you arguing about? (*She shouts.*) Come on, hurry, hurry! Oh, why do you walk so slowly! Where is everyone? What? No, tell me from there. What? [Very stern, did you say?] What about my husband? [My husband!] Where's Anton? Oh! (*She moves away from the window in a fury.*) The man's an imbecile, he won't say a word until he gets inside! (*She paces.*)

    Enter DOBCHINSKY, *out of breath.*

Well? Aren't you ashamed of yourself? I was relying on you, Peter Ivanovich, I thought I could trust you, but no, you had to go dashing off after them and I'm left here all on my own without getting a word out of anyone! Aren't you ashamed? You ask me to be godmother to your children and then you go and treat me like that?

DOBCHINSKY. As God's my judge, I've run myself to a standstill to get here as soon as this! How d'ye do, Maria Antonovna?

MARIA. How do you do, Peter Ivanovich.

ANNA. All right, all right! Tell me what happened. How did things go?

DOBCHINSKY. Anton Antonovich has sent you a note.

ANNA. But what is he? The visitor? Is he a General?

DOBCHINSKY. No, he's not. But he's as good as a General

every bit as good. Better, in fact. He's so cultured! So . . .
impressive!

ANNA. It must be the Inspector that Chmikhov wrote to us
about.

DOBCHINSKY. Oh, no doubt about it! And it was me that
discovered him – me and Peter Ivanovich!

ANNA. But tell us what's *happened*! Quickly!

DOBCHINSKY. Well, at the moment everything seems to be
going smoothly, God be praised. Oh, but he gave poor
Anton Antonovich such a stiff reception to begin with!
Quite furious, he was, complaining about his room and the
food but refusing to come here, and saying he wasn't going
to the prison on any account. But then when he realized
that the bad food, and that, wasn't Anton Antonovich's
fault, and we'd had a bit of a talk, he suddenly calmed down
and everything started going much better, thanks be to
God. They've gone off now to look at the hospital. You
know, for a while Anton Antonovich really did think there'd
been a secret report sent in about him! I was even quite
scared myself!

ANNA. You've nothing to be scared about – you're not even
an official.

DOBCHINSKY. I know, but you can't help shaking a bit when
someone really superior is speaking.

ANNA. None of that's important. The thing is, what's he like?
Is he old or young?

DOBCHINSKY. Quite young, to look at – but he talks like an
old man! 'I'm much obleeged to you, sir . . .' that's the way
he talks . . . 'I'd be delighted to accompany you . . .' (*He
waves his hand vaguely*.) Oh, all terribly high class! 'I'd like
to read and write,' he said to me, 'only this room's so
frightfully dark!'

ANNA. But what's he *like*? To look at, I mean? Is he dark or
fair?

DOBCHINSKY. More sort of yellow . . . or corn-coloured.
And his eyes are quick like a ferret's – they make you feel
very uneasy.

ANNA. Let's see what Anton says. (*She reads*.) 'I scribble this in haste, my dear, just to tell you that my position at first seemed fraught with danger one half portion of caviar but putting my trust in the mercy of God two portions pickled cucumber one-twenty-five . . .' (*She stops.*) I can't understand a word of this, what have pickled cucumbers got to do with it?

DOBCHINSKY. Anton Antonovich scribbled it on the first piece of paper he could find – it's a hotel bill.

ANNA. Oh, yes, it's a bill. (*She goes on reading.*) '. . . hum – hum – the mercy of God, I believe we shall come through safely in the end. You must hurry and get the spare room ready for our distinguished guest. The one with the yellow wallpaper. Don't bother about lunch, we shall have a meal at the hospital, but make sure there's plenty of good wine. [Tell Abdullin to send us the best he's got, or I'll turn his cellar upside down with my own hands!] I kiss your hand, my dear, and remain, yours, Anton Skvoznik Dmukhanovsky.' Heavens above, we must hurry! Mishka! Mishka!

DOBCHINSKY (*running to the door*). Mishka!

ANNA. [How long will they be, Peter Ivanovich?

DOBCHINSKY (*running to the window*). They can't be long now.

ANNA. What! But you said . . . you ran straight here from the Inn! And they've gone to the hospital!

DOBCHINSKY. I did, I did, Anna Andreyevna! But I had to go through the dining room, d'you see, to get out of the Inn, and there was such a lovely smell of roast ham, I thought, if I don't snatch a bite now I won't get any lunch *at all* today.

ANNA. Peter Ivanovich Dobchinsky!

DOBCHINSKY. Then I ran all the way here, truly I did!

ANNA. It's disgusting! The sheer treachery of it!] (*Enter* MISHKA.) Oh, Mishka, now listen, I want you to run to Abdullin's . . . no, wait a minute, I'll give you a note, you're so stupid . . . (*She sits, speaking as she writes.*) I want you to give this to Sidor, tell him to take it down to Abdullin's and bring back the wine at once. When you've done that, you can start cleaning up the spare room, the one with the yellow wallpaper – put a decent bed in there, make sure there's a wash-stand and everything, d'you understand? Here, take this. Now off you go – and hurry!

DOBCHINSKY. Perhaps I'd better be off, Anna Andreyevna. See how things are going . . . you know . . . at the hospital . . .

ANNA. Go on, then, I'm not keeping you. Traitor!

    DOBCHINSKY *slinks out hurriedly.*

Now, Maria, we must think about what we're going to wear. He's from Petersburg, we mustn't give him the chance to laugh up his sleeve at us. You must wear your pale blue with the little flounces, that's the most suitable, and I . . .

MARIA (*wailing*). Oh no, Mamma, not the pale blue, I hate the pale blue! That Lyapkin-Tyapkin girl's always in pale blue, and so is that awful Zemlyanika woman! I shall wear my marigold.

ANNA. Your marigold! Really! When will you learn not to do things just to be contrary? You must wear your blue, because *I'm* going to wear my primrose!

MARIA. Oh, Mamma, please! Primrose doesn't suit you at all. You're not . . .

ANNA. I'm not – what?

MARIA. Not dark enough. You have to have dark eyes to wear primrose.

ANNA. Nonsense, girl! Anyway, I have got dark eyes. They must be dark, otherwise how is it that at cards when I tell my fortune I always get the Queen of Spades?

MARIA. You're much more like the Queen of Hearts, really.

    ANNA *starts bundling* MARIA *out.*

ANNA. Rubbish, girl, absolute rubbish!

    They go off.

(*Off.*) I don't know what you'll think of next! Me, the Queen of Hearts! How ridiculous! (*Business with a mirror – she speculatively studies herself.*)

    The door of the spare room opens and MISHKA *sweeps out some dust.* OSSIP *comes in from the front door carrying a suitcase on his head.*

OSSIP. Where d'you want this?

MISHKA. This way, Dad. In here.

OSSIP. Hold on a tick, let me catch me breath. Whew! Wot a load! Still . . . a sack of fevvers'd feel heavy on an empty belly!

MISHKA. Will that General of yours be here soon?

OSSIP. What General?

MISHKA. Your master, of course.

OSSIP. My master? Did you say 'General'?

MISHKA. Isn't he a General, then?

OSSIP. Oh, yes – he's very general.

MISHKA. Is that so? Is he more important than a General, then, or less?

OSSIP. Oh, more, every time!

MISHKA. Is that right! That's why they're making such a fuss about him, then.

OSSIP. Look here, sonny – I can see you're a bright little lad, so what about rustling me up a bite to eat?

MISHKA. They won't have anything ready for you yet, Dad. You wouldn't want to be eating anything plain – you'll be wanting the same as your master gets.

OSSIP. What would you call something plain?

MISHKA. Well . . . there's some cabbage soup, meat pie, and pudding.

OSSIP. Just you bring me your cabbage soup, meat pie and pudding. I don't mind eating plain for once! Come on, let's get this thing stowed away. Where is it – in here?

MISHKA. This way, then . . . we can go out through the back. . . .

They go off through the side door, carrying the case between them.

The main door is flung open by two POLICEMEN, *who flank the entrance. Enter* KHLYESTAKOV, *followed by the* MAYOR, *the* CHARITY COMMISSIONER, *the* JUDGE, *the* SCHOOLS SUPERINTENDENT, *the* POSTMASTER, *the* POLICE INSPECTOR, DOBCHINSKY *and* BOBCHINSKY – *the latter with a strip of plaster across his nose. The* MAYOR *gestures grandly at a scrap of paper on the floor; both* POLICEMEN *dive for it, and collide in mid-air.*

KHLYESTAKOV (*expansively*). Well, that's a splendid hospital, splendid. I must say I like the way you show your visitors around the town, it really is most civil! No one ever showed me a thing in any of the other dumps I've been in.

MAYOR. I'm afraid that in some towns the officials are too busy looking after their own interests to do their jobs properly. Here, if I may say so, we think only of how we can earn the approval of our superiors by our vigilance, diligence and the proper administration of Government regulations. So help me, God. Mishka!

KHLYESTAKOV. That was a fine lunch we had – I'm sure I ate too much. Do you eat like that here every day?

Enter MISHKA *with a tray of drinks.*

MAYOR. It was specially prepared, Your Honour, for our very welcome guest.

KHLYESTAKOV. I must say I love good food. That's what life is for – to gather the blossoms of pleasure in full bloom! What was that marvellous fish we had?

CHARITY COMMISSIONER (*bobbing up beside* KHLYESTAKOV). That was salted cod, Your Honour.

KHLYESTAKOV. Really? I'd never have believed it! Cod, eh? Delicious. Where was it we lunched – the hospital, was it?

CHARITY COMMISSIONER. That's right, Your Honour.

KHLYESTAKOV. Yes, I remember now, there were some beds standing around, weren't there? Have all your patients recovered, then? There didn't seem to be any about?

CHARITY COMMISSIONER. [Ah, there's no more'n a dozen or so left now, Your Honour, all the rest've recovered completely.] It's all a question of good management. Ever since I took over that hospital – you may not believe this, sir, but it's true – the patients have been recovering like flies. A sick man can hardly set foot in the place before he's out again, completely cured! [It's not so much your medicines and your treatments, more a matter of really honest and efficient administration.]

MAYOR. Ah, yes, but think what a headache it must be when a man's got a whole town to administer! Think of the hundreds of problems a Mayor has to take on his shoulders

– sanitation, maintenance, public order – the ablest of men might find it too much for him, but here, praise be to God, everything's under good control. There's many a Mayor, do you know, would be feathering his own nest – oh, yes! But when I lie in my bed at night, I have only one thought: 'Almighty God,' I think to myself, 'help me to give absolute satisfaction to my superiors!' [I think of nothing else.] Whether they choose to reward me or not, of course, that's their affair. [If I can see a clean, well-cared-for town, the convicts properly looked after, not too many drunks in the streets – there's the satisfaction of a job well done. What more could I want?] I'm not after honours and decorations . . . ! Of course, that sort of thing has its attractions, but as the poet says, compared to the joys of a job well done, everything else is as dust and ashes!

CHARITY COMMISSIONER (*aside*). Listen to him laying it on!

KHLYESTAKOV. Oh, that's all very true! I am myself, I confess, quite fond of philosophizing about this and that – sometimes in prose, and sometimes, d'you know, in verse . . . according to my inspiration.

BOBCHINSKY (*to* DOBCHINSKY). Isn't that nicely put, Peter Ivanovich? The way he speaks, it's so . . . you know, you can tell he's studied a lot, can't you?

KHLYESTAKOV. But tell me, aren't there any entertainments in this town . . . you know, places people can drop into for a hand of cards if they feel like it, that sort of thing?

MAYOR (*aside*). Ah-a! I know what he's driving at! (*Aloud.*) God forbid, sir, that anything like *that* should happen in *my* town! I've never held a playing card in my hand in my life, I wouldn't know what to do with it if I did! [I can't bear the sight of a pack of cards, Your Honour.] Why, if I so much as catch sight of a King of Diamonds, it turns my stomach. [I remember once I thought I'd amuse the children by building a house of cards, and do you know, I dreamed of the damned things all night?] I can't think how people can waste their time on such things!

SCHOOLS SUPERINTENDENT (*aside*). And he took a hundred roubles off me only last night!

MAYOR. I prefer to spend my time serving the State.

KHLYESTAKOV. I think that's going a bit far. It all depends how you look at it. Now, of course, if you make the mistake of backing out just when you ought to be doubling your stakes, then. . . . No, no, I can't agree, it's really very jolly to have a hand of cards now and then. . . .

Enter ANNA *and* MARIA, *resplendent.*

MAYOR. Your Honour, allow me to introduce . . . my wife, and my little daughter.

KHLYESTAKOV (*bowing deeply*). Madam, it is indeed a pleasure, if I may say so, to have the pleasure, as it were, of – er – meeting you!

ANNA (*low curtsey*). Our pleasure is much greater, Your Honour, in having so distinguished a guest!

KHLYESTAKOV (*striking an attitude*). No, 'pon my soul, Madam, on the contrary, my pleasure is far, far greater!

ANNA. Oh, sir, now you're just being polite, I'm sure! Won't you please sit down?

KHLYESTAKOV. Madam, simply to stand in such charming company is joy itself! However, if you insist, I'll sit. (*They sit on the sofa together.*) Ah, what happiness it is for me to be sitting with you beside me!

ANNA. I dare not think your words are anything but politeness, sir! Er . . . I imagine, sir, that life in the country must be very distasteful to you after life in Petersburg?

KHLYESTAKOV. Oh, an unimaginable tediosity, Madam! When one is accustomed, comprenny-vous, to life in the best Society, suddenly to find oneself on the road, living in dirty inns amongst uncultured people . . . ! If it weren't for my good fortune today . . . (*He looks up into* ANNA'*s eyes.*) . . . which, I assure you, makes up for everything . . .

ANNA. It must all be so very unpleasant for you, sir.

KHLYESTAKOV. At this moment, Madam, everything is pleasantness itself!

ANNA. Oh, how can you say such things! I'm not worthy of such compliments!

KHLYESTAKOV. On the contrary, Madam, nobody could be more worthy!

ANNA. But I live in the country. . . .

KHLYESTAKOV. And the country itself has its beauties – the woods, the hills, the sparkling streams. . . . One can't, of course, compare it with Petersburg. . . . Ah, Petersburg! Ça, c'est la vivre! You may be thinking that I'm only a clerk, but let me tell you the head of my department is very friendly with me! He'll slap me on the back, so, and say: 'Come round for dinner, old chap' – just like that! I drop into the office for a few minutes, hand out a few instructions, and leave the old copy-clerk scratching away at his desk. . . . They wanted to promote me, once, but I thought, 'Ah, what's the use?' – and I turned it down. The office porter runs after me with his brush. . . . 'Allow me, Ivan Alexandrovich, allow me! I just want to shine your boots!' (*To the* MAYOR.) Why are you all still standing, gentlemen? Do sit down!

MAYOR.
SCHOOLS SUPERINTENDENT. } We can stand . . . That's all right, Your Honour . . . We know our rank . . .
CHARITY COMMISSIONER.

KHLYESTAKOV. Never mind your rank! Sit down!! (*They all scurry to take a seat.*) I won't have any standing on ceremony! I do everything I can, you know, to escape attention, but I'm afraid it's impossible. Wherever I turn up the word seems to get around at once. 'There goes Ivan Alexandrovich Khlyestakov!' they say. Once I was actually mistaken for the Commander-in-Chief – yes! The soldiers all came dashing out of the guardroom to present arms! And later their officer – who's actually a close friend of mine – said 'D'you know, old chap, everyone was convinced you were the Commander-in-Chief!'

ANNA. Well! Would you believe it!

KHLYESTAKOV. It's quite true. Oh, and I know all the pretty actresses in town, of course. Well, you see, I've done quite a lot of writing for the stage . . . amusing little things . . . I go about a lot in the literary world . . . Pushkin's a close pal of mine. Whenever I see him I say, 'Well, Pushkin, old boy, how're things going with you?' And, do you know, he always says exactly the same thing: 'So-so, old chap,' he says, '. . . only so-so.' Ah, he's a great character, is Pushkin!

ANNA. Are you really a writer, then? Oh, how wonderful it must be to be a writer! Do you ever write for the magazines?

KHLYESTAKOV. Oh, yes, I publish in magazines, too. But then I do so many things: novels, plays . . . *Don Juan*, *Romeo and Juliet*, *The Marriage of Figaro* . . . I really can't remember all the titles. It was sheer chance that they came to be written anyway. Theatre managers were always pestering me – 'Please, old chap, do write something for us, you know you can!' Eventually, just to get rid of them, I thought 'All right, dammit, I will!' And I sat down, and do you know, I scribbled the whole lot in one evening! They were astonished, I can tell you. (*Pause.*) Yes, well, I've always had a very ready wit. All those pieces in *The Moscow Telegraph* under the name of Baron Brambeus – they're all mine.

ANNA. No! Are you really Baron Brambeus?

KHLYESTAKOV. Oh, yes. Why, there's hardly a writer in the country whose work I haven't rewritten for him at one time or another – I get forty thousand a year doing that sort of thing.

ANNA. I've just been reading a novel called *Youri Miloslavsky* –

KHLYESTAKOV. Oh, yes, that's another of mine.

ANNA. I knew it!

MARIA. But Mamma, it says on the cover that it was written by Zagoskin!

ANNA. You would have to argue, wouldn't you?

KHLYESTAKOV. You're quite right, Madam, there is a book of that name by Zagoskin. But there is also one by me.

ANNA. There! And I'm sure it was yours I read – it's so well written!

KHLYESTAKOV. I must admit, I just live for literature! I keep the best house in Petersburg – everyone knows it, Khlyestakov House they call it. (*To them all with a sweep.*) Gentlemen, if you ever come to Petersburg, you must all come and see me! I give the grandest receptions, you know!

ANNA. I can imagine how magnificent they must be!

KHLYESTAKOV. Oh, they're quite indescribable! In the centre of the table there'll be a huge water-melon costing seven hundred roubles. Then I have soup brought straight from Paris, by steamship, in special containers – you lift the lid, and that Parisienne aroma – ah, there's nothing like it in the world! I go to a dance or a reception every day! Sometimes we make up a four for cards – the English Ambassador, the Foreign Minister, the French Ambassador, the German Ambassador . . . and me. Then, when I get tired of playing cards, I dash up to my little fourth-floor flat and my old cook comes out of the kitchen and I say, 'Take my coat, Mavrushka . . .' Oh, no, what nonsense, I live on the first floor, don't I? And that great staircase of mine, it must be worth . . . ah, you should see my reception hall in the morning, buzzing with counts and princes before I'm even awake . . . bzz, bzz, bzz . . . like a lot of bees, they are. . . . Sometimes you'll even find the Prime Minister there, just hanging about, waiting for me . . .

The MAYOR *and the others rise, awestruck.*

My letters are all addressed to 'Your Excellency', because I was once head of a whole Government department! Oh, yes! Very odd, that was. The director suddenly disappeared, no one knew where, and there were the usual squabbles over who should have the post. There were plenty of generals after the job, and some of them tried to do it, but it was no good, one after another they had to go, it was just too difficult. It looked simple enough at first sight, but when you got down to it, it needed real brains. So in the end they had to send for me. 'Send for Ivan Alexandrovich,' they said – and the messengers went out, all over Petersburg, messenger after messenger, all looking for me! Well, imagine it – thirty-five thousand messengers scurrying about, what about that, eh? 'Ivan Alexandrovich,' they cried when they found me, 'come and take charge of the department!' I was staggered, I wanted to refuse, but then I thought, what if the Tsar heard about my refusal, he'd be offended! So I said to them, 'All right,' I said, 'I'll do it,' I said, 'but I warn you, you'll have to watch out with me, I don't stand any nonsense from anyone . . .' And do you know, when I walked through that department you'd have thought there was an earthquake going on, they were all shaking and shivering so much with fear!

The MAYOR, *etc., shiver.* KHLYESTAKOV *gets more excited.*

Oh, I won't be trifled with! I put the fear of God up them! I even had the Privy Council shaking in their shoes! Oh, yes! And why not, eh? That's the sort of man I am, not afraid of anybody. I tell them straight out, 'Don't you try to stand in my way, my man!' And they don't! Because I can go anywhere – anywhere! I'm in and out of the Palace at all hours of the day and night – all hours! Why, tomorrow . . . tomorrow . . . they're going to make me . . . a . . . a Field Marshal!

He slips and almost falls, but the officials very respectfully support him.

MAYOR (*tries to speak but is trembling too much*). Your . . . Your . . . Your . . .

KHLYESTAKOV (*very sharp and abrupt*). Well, what is it, what is it?

MAYOR. Yo-Yo – Your—

KHLYESTAKOV (*more sharply still*). I can't understand a word, you're talking nonsense!

MAYOR. Y-your lexency – elxency – Exclensy . . . m-m-might w-w-want to l-l-lie down, have rest . . . your room's ready here, everything you need. . . .

KHLYESTAKOV. Lie down? Rest? Rubbish! Oh, all right, if you like, I suppose I might . . . that lunch was really very good, gentlemen, I'm much obleeged, much ob-leeged! (*He suddenly declaims.*) Salted Cod! Salted Cod! SALTED COD!

He nearly falls, but is helped out by the MAYOR.

BOBCHINSKY (*to* DOBCHINSKY). What a man, Peter Ivanovich! There you have a real man! [Never in my life have I been in the presence of a person of such real importance!]

I nearly died of fright, didn't you? What's his rank, d'you think?

DOBCHINSKY. Oh, he must be at least a General!

BOBCHINSKY. He must be the Generalissimo himself! [You heard how he bosses the Privy Council about! I bet any General would have to stand to attention in front of a man like him! Come on,] let's all go and tell Fyodorovich and Korobkin all about it! Goodbye, Anna Andreyevna!

DOBCHINSKY. Goodbye, Anna Andreyevna!

Both run out.

CHARITY COMMISSIONER. I'm terrified! I don't quite know why, but I'm simply terrified. We aren't even in proper uniform – there's no knowing what he may do when he wakes up sober! (*He goes thoughtfully to the* SCHOOLS SUPERINTENDENT.) He'll probably dash off a report to Petersburg! Excuse us, Anna Andreyevna!

They go off.

ANNA. What a fascinating man!

MARIA. He's a darling!

ANNA. He's so refined! You can see at once he's a man of fashion! Those lovely manners . . . beautiful gestures! [Gracious me, I do admire young men like that! Such grace and style! And so gallant!] I noticed he couldn't keep his eyes off me!

MARIA. [Oh, Mamma, really!] It was me he was looking at!

ANNA. You? Don't be ridiculous, dear!

MARIA. He was looking at me!

ANNA. [Good God, will the girl never stop contradicting me?] Why should he look at you? Can you tell me one reason on earth why he should look at you?

MARIA. Well, he just did, that's all. When he started talking about his books he stole a glance at me, and I caught his eye. And when he mentioned that game of cards with all those Ambassadors, he was looking straight at me, so there!

ANNA. Well, maybe he did throw you a quick glance, but he was only being polite.

Enter the MAYOR *on tiptoe.*

MAYOR. Sssssh! Sssssh!

ANNA. What's wrong?

MAYOR. I wish I hadn't made him drunk. [I don't know what to think now.] Suppose only half what he said was true? (*He thinks deeply.*) And why shouldn't it be true? When a man's drunk the truth slips out, you can't prevent it. So he plays cards with Ambassadors, he pops in and out of the Palace ... dear God, [my poor head's going to burst at this rate,] I feel like a man on a scaffold, no mistake.

ANNA. I wasn't a bit frightened of him myself. To me he was just a man of real culture and breeding, that's all. I don't give a fig about his rank.

MAYOR. Aaargh! Women! It's nothing but a game to you, is it? You with your silks and satins and feathers and flutters, if you drop a brick all you get is a good hiding from your husband – but your husband gets the sack! Don't you realize you were talking to him the way you talk to any wretched Peter Ivanovich?

ANNA. You worry too much, Antosha. We women know a thing or two, remember. (*She looks meaningfully at* MARIA.)

MAYOR. Ah, what's the use of talking to females!

   He opens the door and calls.

Mishka! Mishka! Run and call those two constables, out by the gate, there.

   Brief silence.

Ah, it's a funny world. You might have expected to see someone impressive to look at, [but a fancy-looking little whipper-snapper like that!] I dunno! Who'd ever have guessed if we hadn't been warned? [And didn't he just lead us a dance at the Inn this morning! But he's given in now, all right – in fact, he's spilled more of the beans than he need have. That'll be on account of him being so young.] But we know where we are now, all right.

   Enter OSSIP.
   They all make a dash at him.

ANNA. Ah! Come here now, my good man ...

MAYOR. Sssh! Ssssh! (*To* OSSIP.) Well? Is he asleep?

OSSIP. Not quite. Just yawning and stretching a bit.

ANNA. Er – hmm – what's your name?

OSSIP. Ossip, Ma'am.

MAYOR. Now that'll do, that'll do! (*To* OSSIP.) Well, old man, have they given you a decent dinner?

OSSIP. Very nice dinner, sir, thank you, sir.

ANNA. Now, tell me . . . I imagine you get quite a few titled people coming to your master's house, eh? Counts and princes, and so on?

OSSIP (*looking round at them with visible cunning*). Oh, yes, Ma'am. All manner of counts and dukes and princes and that.

MARIA. Isn't your master handsome, Ossip! Isn't he?

ANNA. Ossip, tell us what he . . .

MAYOR. That's enough, stop it now! [You're only hindering us with all this stupid questioning! Now, old man, I want you to tell me . . .]

ANNA. What's your master's rank, Ossip?

OSSIP (*cunning again*). Oh, you know – the usual.

MAYOR. God in heaven, how you do keep on!

ANNA (*interrupting*). Ossip, does your master wear uniform at home?

MAYOR. Be quiet, will you? Can't you see this is serious, [it's a matter of life and death.] (*To* OSSIP.) Now I've taken a liking to you, my friend. I know a man likes to have an extra glass of something when he's travelling [– particularly in cold weather –] so here's a couple of roubles I expect you'll find a use for. . . . Go on, hide them away.

OSSIP (*taking the coins*). Very grateful, Your Honour, I'm sure. (*He pulls his forelock.*) May God reward you for helping a poor man, Your Honour.

MAYOR. Not at all, not at all. I'm only too glad to help you. Now then, what sort of things does your master like most when he's travelling, eh?

OSSIP. It all depends, sir, what's available, so to speak. He likes being well-looked-after, and he likes to see I'm well-looked-after too. He's very particular that way. Soon as we've left a place, first thing he asks is, 'Now then, Ossip, did they look after you well back there?' 'No, not very well,' I may say, and that'll be a black mark against them.

But of course, Your Honour, I'm a simple man myself, it's nothing to me.

MAYOR. You're a very good man, Ossip, you talk good sense. I gave you something for a little drink, didn't I? Well, here's something for a bite to eat, as well.

OSSIP. Very kind, Your Honour, I'm sure. (*He puts the money away.*) I'll drink to Your Honour's health.

ANNA. Come and talk to me, Ossip. I've got a little something for you, too!

MARIA (*sighing*). Oh, Ossip . . . kiss your master for me! Will you?

> KHLYESTAKOV *is heard coughing from the next room.*

MAYOR. Ssssh! (*He walks on tiptoe to listen at* KHLYESTAKOV'*s door. The rest of the scene is played in whispers.*) Not a sound, now, d'you hear! Run along now, you two, you've chattered quite enough.

ANNA. Come on then, Mashenka. There's one fascinating thing *I* noticed about our guest . . . I'll tell you as soon as we're alone.

> *She sweeps out,* MARIA *following.*

MAYOR. Talk, talk, talk – women'll talk your ears right off! (*Turning to* OSSIP.) Now, old chap . . .

> *Enter, noisily,* SVISTUNOV *and* DYERZHIMORDA.

Ssssh! You noisy brutes, clumping in here like a cartload of logs, where the devil have you been, then?

DYERZHIMORDA. Sir, acting on superior orders, we was proceeding . . .

MAYOR. Be quiet! (*He claps his hand over* DYERZHIMORDA'*s mouth.*) You bray like a donkey! [(*Imitating.*) 'We was proceeding' . . . Like a damned brass band!] (*To* OSSIP.) All right, old friend, you can run along now and get anything your master needs. Ask for anything you like, the house is yours.

> OSSIP *goes off.*

Now, you two – go and stand by that front door, and don't you move, not one single inch. Don't, [whatever you do,] let anybody in – least of all those damned tradesmen! [You let one of those through and I'll . . . I'll . . . string you up

with my own hands!] If you see one of them coming here
with anything that looks like a petition, you just pick him
up by the scruff and sling him out! Like this, see? (*He
kicks out an imaginary petitioner.*) Off you go, then. Shhhh!
Sssshhh!

He tiptoes out after the CONSTABLES.

CURTAIN

Act Two

SCENE ONE

The same scene, the following morning. Enter, on tiptoe, the JUDGE, *the* CHARITY COMMISSIONER, *the* DISTRICT PHYSICIAN, *the* POSTMASTER, *the* SCHOOLS SUPERINTENDENT, BOBCHINSKY *and* DOBCHINSKY. *All are in full dress uniform. The scene is conducted in a whisper.*

JUDGE. For pity's sake gentlemen, [get a move on,] get into order . . . tallest in the middle, that's right, it's all got to look right and proper, this here's a man visits the Palace ten times a day, remember, tells off the Privy Council, God help us. Stand to attention, dress by the right . . . no, Peter Ivanovich, you go down that end and you, Peter Ivanovich, up this end. There!

 BOBCHINSKY *and* DOBCHINSKY *scurry on tiptoe to their places.*

CHARITY COMMISSIONER. [That's all very well, Amos Fyodorovich, but] I think we ought to make some sort of move . . . do something.

JUDGE. What sort of move?

CHARITY COMMISSIONER. You know what I mean.

JUDGE (*rubbing finger and thumb together*). A bit of . . . ?

CHARITY COMMISSIONER. Why not?

JUDGE. Too dangerous, that's why not. He's an important man, he might raise an awful stink. Though I suppose we could make it look like a – a public subscription for some monument or other?

POSTMASTER. Couldn't we say it was money that came through the post, and has never been collected?

CHARITY COMMISSIONER. You watch he doesn't send you through the post, Ivan Kuzmich – to somewhere cold and far away! No, listen, that's not the way things are done in a well-ordered society. What are we all doing here *together* like this, eh? We ought to be paying our respects one at a time. Then, when we've each got him alone . . . well, no one's any the wiser, are they? That's the way things are done. And I think you ought to go first, Amos Fyodorovich!

JUDGE. Me? Oh, no, it'd be better for you to go first, he's already broken bread with you, remember.

CHARITY COMMISSIONER. That's exactly why I shouldn't go first. No, I think it should be Luka Lukich. After all, he represents knowledge and enlightenment and that.

SCHOOLS SUPERINTENDENT. I couldn't. No, gentlemen, really, I couldn't! [It's my training.] Soon as anyone even a single grade above me starts speaking, I curl up inside from fright and swallow my tongue! No, I'm sorry, gentlemen, you'll have to excuse me, I can't do it!

CHARITY COMMISSIONER. Well, then, it'll just have to be you, Amos Fyodorovich. You're the one with the silver tongue, you speak just like Cicero.

JUDGE. Cicero, indeed! Just because I get a bit worked up when we're talking about shooting . . .

ALL. Not just shooting . . . !
    You can talk about anything . . . !
    You can do it, Amos Fyodorovich . . . !
    Don't let us down . . . !
    Yes, yes, you must be first . . . !

JUDGE. Please, let me alone, gentlemen! Please!
    At this moment there are sounds from the room where KHLYESTAKOV *is sleeping. They all scramble for the door, trampling each other as they go.*

ALL. [Ow, Peter Ivanovich! That's my toe . . . !
    Careful, you're killing me . . . !
    Let me out . . . I'm being squashed to death . . . !
    Ouch . . . ! Help . . . ! Let me through . . . !
    At last the stage is empty.]
    Enter, very slowly, a sleepy KHLYESTAKOV.

KHLYESTAKOV. Whew, what a sleep, I must have been out for hours! Where do they get these feather beds, I wonder?

I'm roasted alive! God knows what they gave me to drink
yesterday – my head's still buzzing like a hornet's nest. . . .
Still, it looks as if I could have a good time here, they're
all very hospitable and they seem to do it out of pure kind-
ness of heart, which makes a nice change. . . . That girl,
the daughter, isn't a bad little chick . . . and I wouldn't be
surprised if the old hen herself had a squawk left in her . . .
hmm . . . yes, I must say I rather fancy life in this place.

    Enter the JUDGE.

JUDGE (*hovering by the door; aside*). God help me, my knees
are giving way!

    He draws himself up and puts his hand on his sword.

I have the honour of introducing myself, Your Excellency.
Lyapkin-Tyapkin, Civil Captain First Class, Commissioner
for Oaths, Judge of the District Court of this town!

KHLYESTAKOV. Ah . . . is that so? Well – er – sit down, won't
you? So you're the Judge here, are you?

JUDGE. Elected in 1816 for a three-year term, Your Honour.
I have held the post ever since.

KHLYESTAKOV. Really? Quite a – profitable post, I suppose –
being Judge in a place like this?

JUDGE (*embarrassed*). After nine years, sir, I was awarded
the Order of St Vladimir, Fourth Class. (*Aside.*) Dear God,
the money's burning a hole in my hand!

KHLYESTAKOV. I like the Vladimir ribbon – much prettier
than the St Anne, don't you think . . . ?

JUDGE (*advancing his fist a little*). God a'mercy, I feel like a
cat on hot bricks!

KHLYESTAKOV. What's that you've got in your hand?

JUDGE (*jumps, dropping the notes*). What! Nothing! No,
nothing at all!

KHLYESTAKOV. Nothing? But you've dropped a lot of
money!

JUDGE (*shaking all over*). Oh – er – no – er – not at all! (*Aside.*)
Oh, my God, now I've done it!

KHLYESTAKOV (*picking up the money*). You have, you know.
It's money, look!

JUDGE (*aside*). I'm lost – done for – finished!

KHLYESTAKOV. Look here, Judge, I wonder if you'd mind lending me this . . . just a short loan . . . ?

JUDGE (*quickly*). Oh, of course, of course, with pleasure, sir! (*Aside.*) Holy Mary, I'm saved!

KHLYESTAKOV. What with one thing and another I find my travels have run me short of ready money . . . I'll let you have it back, of course, as soon as I reach my estate.

JUDGE. Please, please, Your Honour, don't give it a thought, it's a pleasure, it's a . . . I – I do my best, Your Honour, to serve . . . obey . . . as far as lies . . . as far as I lie . . . as far as in me lies . . . to serve . . . (*He staggers up from his chair and stands to attention.*) I will not disgrace Your Excellency's presence any longer. Does Your Excellency have any instructions for me?

KHLYESTAKOV. Instructions?

JUDGE. About the District Court?

KHLYESTAKOV. Good Lord, no! Why should I . . . (*He thinks.*) No, there's no instructions. Not just now, anyway. Thanks all the same.

JUDGE (*bowing and scraping his way out; aside*). God be praised, the battle's won! (*He goes off.*)

KHLYESTAKOV. Seems quite a civil fellow – for a Judge.

Enter the POSTMASTER, *rigidly erect, his hand tight on his sword.*

POSTMASTER. I have the honour, sir, to present myself: Shpyokin, Civil Officer Sixth Class and Postmaster.

KHLYESTAKOV. Pleased to meet you, I'm sure. Do sit down. Well – er – I suppose you've always lived around here, have you?

POSTMASTER. That's right, sir.

KHLYESTAKOV. I must say, I like the place. It's not very big, of course, but then it's not supposed to be a capital city, is it? No . . .

POSTMASTER. No, sir. That's quite right, sir.

KHLYESTAKOV. Of course, it's only in the capital that you find the *bon ton* – and can avoid all these dreary provincials. Isn't that so?

POSTMASTER. Oh, yes, yes, indeed, certainly! (*Aside.*) He's not a bit snobbish . . . wants my opinion about everything!

KHLYESTAKOV. Still, there's no reason why people shouldn't be happy even in a small town, is there?

POSTMASTER. No. Er – no, sir, quite correct.

KHLYESTAKOV. I mean – what do people need? Really *need*, to be happy? They just want to be liked and respected by their fellow men, don't they? Anyway, that's what I think.

POSTMASTER. You're absolutely right, Your Honour.

KHLYESTAKOV. I'm delighted you agree. You know, lots of people think I'm a bit odd, but there, that's the way I am. (*Aside.*) Wonder if I can touch this one for a loan, too? (*Aloud.*) D'you know, the oddest thing happened to me the other day. At the last town I stopped at I lost absolutely *all* my money! Every single kopek! Imagine! I suppose you couldn't by any chance lend me three hundred roubles, could you?

POSTMASTER. What? Oh, yes, certainly, with the greatest of pleasure. There you are, sir – three hundred. Very happy to be of service, Your Honour.

KHLYESTAKOV. Very grateful, old chap. I hate running myself short when I'm travelling, don't you know. Anyway, why should I, eh? Why should I?

POSTMASTER. No, indeed, sir, absolutely! (*He draws himself up stiffly.*) I won't trouble Your Excellency any further . . . unless Your Honour has some instructions . . . ?

KHLYESTAKOV. No, no, none at all, old chap.

(*The* POSTMASTER *bows himself out, muttering 'Thank you, Your Honour, thank you, thank you . . .'*)

The Postmaster seems to be a decent sort of chap too. Most obliging. (*He counts his takings.*)

The SCHOOLS SUPERINTENDENT *is shoved into the room, shaking like a leaf; he masters himself, clutches his sword, and advances.*

SCHOOLS SUPERINTENDENT (*gabbling*). Beg the honour introduce self – Khlopov Civil Off. Sec. Class, Super-'ten' Schools!

KHLYESTAKOV. Ah, good, delighted! Sit down, sit down! Have a cigar, old chap?

SCHOOLS SUPERINTENDENT (*aside*). Oh, God, do I take it
. . . or don't I?

KHLYESTAKOV. Come on, come on, take it! It's not a bad
one – nothing to the ones we get in Petersburg, of course, –
I pay twenty-five roubles a hundred for mine, but they're
worth every kopek. Here, light up! (*He offers a light; the*
SCHOOLS SUPERINTENDENT *is trembling so much he can't
get the cigar near the flame.*) That's the wrong end, old boy.
    The SCHOOLS SUPERINTENDENT, *panic-stricken, drops
    the cigar.*
I can see you're no cigar-lover, old chap.

SCHOOLS SUPERINTENDENT (*aside*). Oh, migawd, I've
ruined everything now!

KHLYESTAKOV. They're one of my weaknesses, I'm afraid.
The other one is (*He leans forward.*) – women! Ah! I just
can't resist a pretty woman! How about you, eh? What
d'you fancy – blondes or brunettes, eh? Oh, come on
now . . .

SCHOOLS SUPERINTENDENT. I daren't venture to have an
opinion, Your Honour.

KHLYESTAKOV. Don't try to wriggle out of it, now! I want
to know!

SCHOOLS SUPERINTENDENT. If I may make so bold, sir,
perhaps . . . I might venture to suggest . . . (*Aside.*) God
Almighty, what am I talking about . . . ?

KHLYESTAKOV. You won't tell me, will you? I think it's
those little brunettes that you fancy, isn't it? Come on now,
own up, you do! (*The* SCHOOLS SUPERINTENDENT *is
speechless.*) Ha! You're blushing! Yes, you are! I was right,
wasn't I? Why wouldn't you say?

SCHOOLS SUPERINTENDENT. I was . . . overawed . . . Your
Excel . . . Your Hon . . . Excellency . . . (*Aside.*) Oh, this
damned tongue of mine!

KHLYESTAKOV. Overawed, eh? Yes, well, there is something
about me that inspires awe, I'm often being told that. There
isn't a woman in the world can hold out against me when
I'm really trying, do you know that?

SCHOOLS SUPERINTENDENT. I'm sure they can't, sir.

KHLYESTAKOV. Yes. Well. Look – er – something damned awkward's happened to me. On my way here I somehow managed to run out of cash completely . . . you don't happen to be able to lend me three hundred roubles, do you?

SCHOOLS SUPERINTENDENT (*searching his pockets feverishly; aside*). Oh, God, I've lost it, I've lost it . . . ! No, here it is! (*To* KHLYESTAKOV.) There! Three hundred!
He hands over the notes, shaking with fear.

KHLYESTAKOV. Splendid. Thanks a lot.

SCHOOLS SUPERINTENDENT (*stands, clutching his sword*). I won't impose on Your Honour a moment longer. Except to say . . . to say . . . to say . . .

KHLYESTAKOV (*counting the notes*). Goodbye, then!

SCHOOLS SUPERINTENDENT (*aside, as he scuttles out*). Thank God for that! With a bit of luck he won't want to look at the school at all! (*He goes off.*)
Enter the CHARITY COMMISSIONER, *erect and bland.*

CHARITY COMMISSIONER. May I have the honour of presenting myself, Your Excellency? Zemlyanika, Civil Captain Third Class and Commissioner of Charities.

KHLYESTAKOV. How d'you do? Sit down, please.

CHARITY COMMISSIONER. I had the great honour and pleasure of receiving Your Excellency at the hospital yesterday, [and of showing you personally round the charitable institutions in my charge.]

KHLYESTAKOV. So you did. That was an excellent lunch you gave me, too!

CHARITY COMMISSIONER. I am happy at all times to put myself at the service of my country.

KHLYESTAKOV. Good food is a weakness of mine, you know. (*He looks at the* CHARITY COMMISSIONER *closely.*) You know, you seem a bit taller today than you were yesterday.

CHARITY COMMISSIONER. That's quite possible. (*A brief silence.*) I never spare myself, sir, when serving the state. (*Another silence. He inches his chair forward.*) Which is more than can be said, I'm afraid, for the Postmaster. He never does a stroke. Everything gets held up, letters, documents, everything . . . ! And the Judge – [he uses that courtroom of his as a kennel!] He may be a relation of mine but I must say his general conduct is really scandalous! Scandalous!

KHLYESTAKOV. Is that a fact?

CHARITY COMMISSIONER (*coming closer*). There's a land-owner here, name of Dobchinsky – [Your Excellency saw him yesterday, I think] – soon as this poor Dobchinsky leaves his house, that Judge pops straight in the back door to see Dobchinsky's wife! True as I sit here, sir! Not one of those little Dobchinsky children looks like Dobchinsky, you'll see that for yourself! Every one of 'em, even the little girl, poor thing, looks like the Judge!

KHLYESTAKOV. Is that so? I'd never have thought it of him!

CHARITY COMMISSIONER (*closer still*). And that Superinten-dent of Schools . . . it's a total mystery how that one got himself appointed! Why, he's no better than an anarchist, and that school of his is a hotbed of revolution. If Your Excellency so desires, I'll put all this down in writing.

KHLYESTAKOV. Yes, you do that, will you? I like to have something amusing to read when I'm bored. What did you say your name was?

CHARITY COMMISSIONER. Zemlyanika.

KHLYESTAKOV. Ah, yes. (*Pause.*) Do you have any children?

CHARITY COMMISSIONER. I have five, Your Excellency, [– two already grown up.

KHLYESTAKOV. Two grown up? Really? And – er – what are they – er?

CHARITY COMMISSIONER. Their names, Your Excellency?] Nikolai, Ivan, Elizabeta, Marya and Perpetua!

KHLYESTAKOV. Oh, splendid! Congratulations!

CHARITY COMMISSIONER. I won't take up any more of your time, Your Excellency . . . (*Rising.*) I'm sure you have more urgent duties . . . (*Bowing himself out.*)

KHLYESTAKOV. Not at all, not at all, it's all been most interesting, you must come and have another chat with me some time, I'm extremely fond of . . . (*The* CHARITY COMMISSIONER *is fast vanishing.*) Oh – er – what did you say your name was?

CHARITY COMMISSIONER. Artemy Philipovich Zemlyanika.

KHLYESTAKOV. Well, look here, Artemy Philipovich, the damnedest thing's happened to me – I've been cleaned out of cash ... cleaned right out! I suppose you couldn't lend me – er – say, four hundred ... ?

CHARITY COMMISSIONER (*resigned*). Here you are. Three ... four hundred.

KHLYESTAKOV. Oh, I say, isn't that lucky? Thank you so much, my dear chap!

The CHARITY COMMISSIONER *goes off.*

Enter BOBCHINSKY *and* DOBCHINSKY.

BOBCHINSKY. I have the honour of introducing myself – Peter Ivanovich Bobchinsky, resident of this town and landowner.

DOBCHINSKY. Peter Ivanovich Dobchinsky, landowner and – er – resident of this town.

KHLYESTAKOV. I've met you both, haven't I? (*To* BOB-CHINSKY.) [Aren't you the one that fell through the door?] How's your nose today?

BOBCHINSKY. Please don't concern yourself, Excellency. God be praised, it's quite healed.

KHLYESTAKOV. I'm delighted to hear it. (*He suddenly rounds on them.*) Have you got any money on you?

DOBCHINSKY. Money?

BOBCHINSKY. Money!

KHLYESTAKOV. A thousand roubles or so. As a loan.

BOBCHINSKY. A thousand? Before God, Your Excellency, I've nothing like that? Have you, Peter Ivanovich?

DOBCHINSKY. Certainly not. All my money's in State Bonds, I assure you.

KHLYESTAKOV. Well, if you haven't a thousand, can you let me have a hundred?

BOBCHINSKY (*fumbling in his pockets*). Haven't you got a hundred roubles, Peter Ivanovich? All I've got is forty.

DOBCHINSKY (*searching*). I've got twenty-five.

BOBCHINSKY. Have another look. I know you've got a hole in your righthand pocket – something may have slipped down into the lining.

DOBCHINSKY (*feeling*). There's nothing there, I'm afraid.

KHLYESTAKOV. Don't bother, please, I just thought I'd ask. Sixty-five will do for the moment . . . (*He takes it.*)

DOBCHINSKY. Er-hum. Sir. I wish to take the liberty of asking your advice in a very – um – delicate matter.

KHLYESTAKOV. Ask away, old chap.

DOBCHINSKY. It's – er – very delicate. My son, do you see, was born to me before my marriage.

KHLYESTAKOV. Yes . . . ?

DOBCHINSKY (*embarrassed*). Well, in a manner of speaking, that is. It's just that we had – er – part of the marriage before the marriage, if you follow, sir. [Then afterwards, of course, it was made proper, the full ties of matrimony and everything.] But I want my son to have my name – Dobchinsky – instead of his mother's, do you see?

KHLYESTAKOV. Naturally. There's no difficulty, is there? Let him be called Dobchinsky!

DOBCHINSKY. I wouldn't bother you with this, Excellency, except he's such a very gifted boy! [He knows lots of poems by heart, and only let him get hold of a knife, he does the most remarkable carvings.] Isn't that so, Peter Ivanovich?

BOBCHINSKY. He's very talented, Excellency.

KHLYESTAKOV. Good, delighted to hear it! I'll put in a word for you in the proper quarters. Yes, yes, yes . . . (*He turns to* BOBCHINSKY.) And is there anything I can do for you?

BOBCHINSKY. Yes, indeed, Excellency. A humble request.

KHLYESTAKOV. Well? What is it?

BOBCHINSKY. When you go back to Petersburg, Excellency, I humbly beg you should say to these grand people, these admirals and senators and that, say to them, 'Your Grace . . . your Serenity . . .' or whatever it is '. . . in this little town there lives a man called Peter Ivanovich Bobchinsky!' Just you tell them that: 'There lives a man called Peter Ivanovich Bobchinsky!'

KHLYESTAKOV. All right.

BOBCHINSKY. And if you should happen to meet the Tsar, Excellency, you say to him, 'Do you know, Your Imperial Majesty, in this little town there lives a man called Peter Ivanovich Bobchinsky!'

KHLYESTAKOV. All right.

DOBCHINSKY. Please excuse us for bothering you with our presence.

BOBCHINSKY. Please excuse us for bothering you with our presence.

KHLYESTAKOV. Not at all, it's been a pleasure. (*He shows them out.*) All these poor boobies seem to have taken me for some sort of Government official. I must have spun them a hell of a line yesterday. What an army of dimwits! I must write and tell Tyapichkin about them. He could put them into one of those funny articles of his . . . Hey! Ossip!

He begins writing the letter – saying the words as he writes them:

'My dear Tyapichkin, the most extraordinary things have been happening to me . . .' (*He giggles.*) . . . What a laugh! Just let Tyapichkin get his teeth into this lot. He's a man wouldn't spare his own father to make a good joke. One thing about all these fools, they're good-natured. All this cash! Let's see, now . . . three hundred from that Judge, another three from the Postmaster . . . six, seven, eight hundred . . . agh, what a filthy note! . . . my life, that's over a thousand! Just let me meet that rotten infantry captain again, I'll take him . . . !

Enter OSSIP.

Well, stupid, you see how these people receive me, eh? (*He goes on writing.*)

OSSIP (*sees the money*). Yes, sir, praise be to God. But may I say something, Ivan Alexandrovich?

KHLYESTAKOV. Hm?

OSSIP. The sooner we skip, the better. We best be gone soon.

KHLYESTAKOV (*keeps on writing*). Nonsense! Why?

OSSIP. [That's the way it is, sir. God bless 'em.] They've given us two good days, that's as much as we can expect. No point in hanging about . . . let's get out while we can. [Our luck'll change if we don't, sir, you mark my words.] They've got some lovely horses here; we could be away like the wind.

KHLYESTAKOV (*writing*). I want to stay a bit longer, Ossip. Perhaps we'll go tomorrow.

OSSIP. Tomorrow's too late! Honest to God, sir, why don't we go now? They're making a fine old fuss of you at the moment, but that's all on account of they've mistaken you for some sort of high official from Petersburg.

KHLYESTAKOV. I know!

OSSIP. It can't last. And your father isn't half going to be wild with you taking so long to get home! They've got these lovely horses here, it'd be a shame to waste 'em!

KHLYESTAKOV. All right, all right, all right! But I want this letter to go off first, you can order your lovely horses at the same time. [See we get the best, Ossip! Tell the drivers I'll give them each a silver rouble if they drive like gods and sing like angels . . .] (*He goes on writing.*) Tyapichkin's going to die laughing when he reads this . . .

OSSIP. I'll get one of the men here to take it, sir. I'd best start on the packing.

KHLYESTAKOV. All right. But bring me a candle, Ossip.

OSSIP (*going out – off*). Hey! You! We've got a letter here for the post. [You can tell the Postmaster it doesn't need a stamp, it's official. And tell the stables to send round the best horses they've got – the express team. Tell 'em they needn't worry about the money, the Ministry pays. And tell 'em to get moving, or my master'll be angry! All right, hold on then, the letter's not ready yet.]

KHLYESTAKOV (*writing*). Where's he living now? Is it still Post Office Street? He flits about so much . . . cheaper than paying rent, I suppose. . . . Oh, I'll chance it . . . (*Addressing the letter.*) 'Tyapichkin, Post Office Street . . .'

    OSSIP *brings a candle, and* KHLYESTAKOV *seals his letter. He gives it to* OSSIP.

There you are.

    The voices of the SHOPKEEPERS *are heard off.*

DYERZHIMORDA (*off*). [Hey, who d'you think you're shoving? I've got orders not to let anyone in here!]

SHOPKEEPERS (*off*). Let us in!

        You can't keep us out!

We're going in!

We've got business here . . . !

DYERZHIMORDA (*off*). Move along now, come on, he's not seeing anybody now. He's asleep. Move along there, please!

The noise gets worse.

KHLYESTAKOV. What's all the noise, Ossip? [See what's going on, will you?]

OSSIP. There's a lot of people trying to get in, all waving bits of paper. I think it's you they want to see.

KHLYESTAKOV (*going to the window*). Well, my friends, what is it? What do you want?

SHOPKEEPERS (*off*). We appeal to Your Excellency!

Tell them to let us through!

We have a petition, Your Honour!

KHLYESTAKOV. Let 'em in! Let 'em all in! Go on, Ossip, go and tell the constable to let them come in!

OSSIP *goes off*.

KHLYESTAKOV (*receives petitions through the window.*) 'To His Most Noble Reverence, the Master of Finance [from Abdullin General Stores and Grain merchant . . .'] Master of Finance . . . there's no such title! What the devil's all this about?

OSSIP *shepherds in the* SHOPKEEPERS.

Well, my friends, what can I do for you?

FIRST SHOPKEEPER. We humbly beg your gracious favour, noble lord!

KHLYESTAKOV. But what is it you want?

SECOND SHOPKEEPER. Don't let us be ruined, Your Honour!

THIRD SHOPKEEPER. Save us from this oppression, Your Highness!

KHLYESTAKOV. Who's oppressing you?

ABDULLIN. It's the Mayor, Your Honour! There's never been a Mayor like him, that's a fact. [A man can't tell the things that Mayor'll do to us poor tradesmen. He billets the soldiers on us till we're all but ruined. He insults every last one of us. He pulls our beards and calls us peasants and gypsies. It's not right, Your Honour.] We're respectable citizens, we always do what's needed, he gets what's his due

[–none of us'll kick at handing over a bit of cloth for his wife or his daughter,] but sir, that man's never satisfied! He'll walk into your shop and take the first thing his eye lights on. 'That's a nice bit of cloth,' he'll say, 'send it round to my place . . .' And of course we have to send it round!

KHLYESTAKOV. Tst, tst, tst! What a scoundrel, eh?

FIRST SHOPKEEPER. [No one can remember a Mayor like him, Your Honour.] We have to hide everything in the shop, soon as we see him coming! [T'in't as if it was only the delicacies he was after.] Nothing's safe from him! [Some rubbishy old prunes as've been mouldering in the barrel these past seven year, what no errand boy'd look at, he'll shove his great fist in that barrel.

SECOND SHOPKEEPER. We're generous enough to him on his name day, Your Honour, but that one's not satisfied with one name day, he has to celebrate every Saint in the calendar, so he do!

KHLYESTAKOV. He sounds like a regular brigand!

THIRD SHOPKEEPER. So he is, sir!]

ABDULLIN. But we don't dare complain, Your Honour. He'll billet a whole regiment on you if he finds out, or close down your business. ['I can't have you flogged or tortured,' he'll say, 'that's against the law, but I can see you eat nothing but salt herrings for the rest of your life!']

KHLYESTAKOV. The man's a monster! He ought to be sent straight to Siberia!

ABDULLIN. Ah, that'd do, or anywhere else Your Excellency likes to send him, just so's it's a long way off! Now, sir, Your Excellency won't scorn our humble offerings . . . just this sack of sugar here, and a basket of wine . . .

KHLYESTAKOV. I'm sorry, I couldn't possibly accept them – what can you be thinking of me! I never accept bribes, my friends! However . . . I seem to be a little short of cash . . . if you happened to be in a position to make me a small loan . . . say three hundred roubles . . . a loan is something I can accept.

ALL. Of course, by all means!
     Please accept more, Your Excellency!

Take five hundred, sir . . .

. . . just to please us!

KHLYESTAKOV. Well, I've nothing against a small loan, thank you, thank you . . .

ABDULLIN *offers the money on a silver salver.*

ABDULLIN. Please, Your Honour, won't you take the salver as well?

KHLYESTAKOV. If you insist, I suppose I could take that.

SECOND SHOPKEEPER (*bowing*). Won't you take the sugar too, Your Honour?

KHLYESTAKOV. I'm sorry. I can't accept bribes . . .

OSSIP. Oh, come on, why not, Your Honour? A bit of sugar can come in very handy on the road, you know. Here, I'll take them, put the sugar over here, and the wine. . . . What's that you got there? A bit of rope, is it – here, let's have that too, rope's always useful when you're travelling, for lashing things up and so on . . .

ABDULLIN. Please help us, Your Serenity! If you don't do anything about the Mayor after all this, we might as well all drown ourselves, we'll be finished for good!

KHLYESTAKOV. Of course, my friends, of course, I'll do everything I can!

The SHOPKEEPERS *go off. A* WOMAN's *voice is heard, off.*

VOICE. That's enough of your pushing, now! I'll tell His Excellency on you! Stop shoving, you're hurting!

KHLYESTAKOV. Who's that now? (*He goes to the window.*) What is it, woman, what's the trouble?

VOICES OF TWO WOMEN. Mercy, Your Honour!

Give us a hearing, sir!

Tell them to let us in!

Etc. . . .

KHLYESTAKOV. [Let them in then, Constable.]

The LOCKSMITH's WIFE *and the* SERGEANT's WIDOW *enter.*

LOCKSMITH'S WIFE (*bowing to the floor*). Have mercy on us, Your Honour!

SERGEANT'S WIDOW (*same bow*). Have mercy on us, Your Honour!

KHLYESTAKOV. Why? Who are you?

LOCKSMITH'S WIFE. Petrova Poshlyopkin, my husband's the locksmith, he was . . .

SERGEANT'S WIDOW. Ivanovna, the Sergeant's widow. I was . . .

KHLYESTAKOV. Wait a minute, one at a time! (*To the* LOCKSMITH's WIFE.) Now then, what is it?

LOCKSMITH'S WIFE. It's the Mayor, Your Honour, God rot him. [I pray God to fill his whole filthy family with pesky diseases, all his children and brothers and uncles and aunts and the whole rotten lot of them, may they all stink in hell!

KHLYESTAKOV. Why? What on earth has he done?]

LOCKSMITH'S WIFE. Sent my husband off to the army, that's what, your Honour! And him a married man, that's against the law!

KHLYESTAKOV. [How could he do that, then?

LOCKSMITH'S WIFE. Oh, he could do it, all right, the lousy hog, may God blast him with boils in this world and the next! May his flesh drop off with the plague, and his aunt's filthy flesh too, and his rotten father's stinking flesh too, if he's got a father, which I doubt, please God let them all die horribly and burn forever in hell.] He should have taken that tailor's son, [he's nothing but a nasty little drunk,] only his parents could afford a nice big bribe, [so he picks on the draper's son instead but she – that's his mother, she's a widow – sends three bolts of good linen to the Mayor's wife, so then he comes to me. 'What good's a husband to you,' he says, 'he's no more use as a husband,' he says. 'Well,' says I, 'that's my business whether he's any use or not, I'm the only one as knows that,' I says. 'But he's a thief,' he says, 'perhaps he hasn't stolen anything yet,' he says, 'but he will soon,' he says, 'and then he'll be sent for a soldier anyway,' he says.] I'm only a woman, Your Honour, what'll I do without a man around the house?

KHLYESTAKOV. All right, all right, that'll do . . . !

LOCKSMITH'S WIFE. [Please, sir, don't desert us, please do something . . .]

KHLYESTAKOV (*to the* SERGEANT'*s* WIDOW). And what about you, then?

SERGEANT'S WIDOW. It's the Mayor, sir.

KHLYESTAKOV. Yes, of course. But what about him?

SERGEANT'S WIDOW. He had me flogged, sir.

KHLYESTAKOV (*interested*). Really?

SERGEANT'S WIDOW. [It was all wrong, Your Honour. Some of the women was fighting in the market, and the police didn't get there 'til it was all over. And that man picked on me for no reason, he had them give me such a thrashing] I couldn't sit down for two days, Your Honour!

KHLYESTAKOV. I don't see I can do much about that now.

The SERGEANT'*s* WIDOW *and the* LOCKSMITH'*s* WIFE *speak together.*

SERGEANT'S WIDOW. I know you can't undo what's done, Your Honour, but you could make that rascal pay me damages, couldn't you? I don't have much luck, Your Honour, I might as well try where I can . . . a few roubles would come in very handy just now . . .

LOCKSMITH'S WIFE. That stinking swindling louse, I hope all his children and his grandchildren die at birth and if he's got any in-laws, God make them die slowly . . .

KHLYESTAKOV (*shutting them up*). Very well! I'll see to it, don't worry! . . . You can run along now . . . (*He shoos them out.*)

Hands holding petitions are thrust through the window. Hubbub outside.

KHLYESTAKOV. What the hell's happening out there? (*He goes to the window.*) No, I don't want them, take them away! Go away all of you, I don't want your petitions! (*He leaves the window.*) Ossip, get rid of them, for God's sake, I'm sick of the lot of them! Don't let any more in! (*At the window.*) All right, shove off, the lot of you. Go on, buzz! Come back tomorrow!

The door opens and a battered man in a shabby coat, his lip swollen and his face bandaged, unshaven, miserable, hovers in the entrance; behind him, many more similar figures can be seen.

OSSIP. Here, outside, you! Come on, out!

    OSSIP *shoves the man back into the crowd and follows him out, closing the door behind him. Enter, from the inner door,* MARIA.

KHLYESTAKOV (*calling off*). Ossip! The horses!

MARIA (*girlishly startled*). Oh!

KHLYESTAKOV. Why so frightened, may I ask?

MARIA. I wasn't frightened, really . . .

KHLYESTAKOV. Allow me to say, dear lady, I would be delighted to think you might have thought I would think that you . . . hrchm . . . (*Striking an attitude.*) May I ask where you were going?

MARIA. Why, I wasn't going anywhere, really.

KHLYESTAKOV. And why were you not going anywhere, really, dear lady?

MARIA. I thought perhaps Mamma was in here.

KHLYESTAKOV. Of course. But your real reason . . . ?

MARIA (*hedging*). I'm being a nuisance. I'm sure you've got some awfully important business to attend to.

KHLYESTAKOV (*posturing again*). What business could ever be as important to me, dear lady, as looking into your incomparable eyes? You couldn't possibly be a nuisance, your presence could only be a pleasure!

MARIA. The way you talk! Just like real society!

KHLYESTAKOV. To such a gorgeous creature as yourself, how else should I talk? May I have the extreme happiness of offering you a chair? Only you should have not a simple chair, but a throne!

MARIA. I don't know. I think I ought to be going. (*But she sits down.*)

KHLYESTAKOV. What a beautiful scarf you're wearing!

MARIA. Oh! Go on, you're making fun of me! Just because I'm a provincial . . . !

KHLYESTAKOV. How I would love to be that scarf, nestling so closely round your lily-white neck.

MARIA. What are you talking about? Wanting to be a scarf . . . ! What strange weather we're having today.

KHLYESTAKOV. Your lips, dear lady, are stranger and more inscrutably fascinating than any weather!

MARIA. [Really, the things you say!] Won't you write some verses for my album – I'm sure you know lots of verses, don't you?

KHLYESTAKOV. For you – I could do anything. Ask, and it will be done! What sort of verses would you like?

MARIA. Something . . . well, you know, something good. Something new.

KHLYESTAKOV. Oh, verses, verses . . . I know so many of them!

MARIA. Won't you recite some, then?

KHLYESTAKOV. But why? I can write them down without all that.

MARIA. I'm fond of listening to poems. . . .

KHLYESTAKOV. Well, I know dozens of them, dozens.

MARIA. Well, go on!

KHLYESTAKOV. Well, if you insist, here's one of mine I might put in your album—
    'Shall I compare thee to a summer's day?
    Thou art more lovely and more temperate;
    Rough winds do shake de dum de dum de dum'
And so on and so forth – that's one of my sonnets. I've done lots more, lots, I just can't remember the words this instant. Oh, but what do poems matter, I'd much rather speak of the love I feel when I gaze into your beautiful eyes . . . (*He draws his chair closer to hers.*)

MARIA. Love! Oh, I don't know anything about that. [I don't even know what the word means. . . .] (*She edges her chair away.*)

KHLYESTAKOV (*moving up again*). Why do you move away? It's much nicer being close together!

MARIA (*moving away*). I think it's nicer (*She shifts.*) further (*She shifts.*) away.

KHLYESTAKOV (*closer*). But there's no need to move away. You only imagine we're close. You could just as well imagine we're far apart. Ah, but how happy I would be, dear lady, if I could enfold you in my arms . . .

MARIA (*looking suddenly out of the window*). Oh, look! What sort of bird was that? Was it a magpie?

KHLYESTAKOV (*kissing her shoulder*). Here's a magpie!

MARIA (*jumping up indignantly*). No, really, that's too much!

KHLYESTAKOV (*holding her back*). Forgive me, Ma'am, please forgive me! It was only my great love made me do it, only my love . . .

MARIA. You think just because I'm a country girl you can . . . (*She tries to get away.*)

KHLYESTAKOV (*still holding her*). No! It was love, I swear to you, I meant no harm, it was only my unconquerable love! Oh, forgive me, forgive me, Maria Antonovna, I'll go down on my knees to you if you'll forgive me! (*He falls on his knees.*) Look, look, I'm on my knees before you!
    Enter ANNA ANDREYEVNA.

ANNA. Well! This is a surprise! (*To* MARIA.) What does all this mean, then? That's a fine way to behave, I'm sure!

MARIA. Really, Mamma, it wasn't . . .

ANNA. Leave the room this instant! Go on, run along! And don't you dare show your face in here again! (MARIA *goes off in tears.*) I'm sorry, Your Honour, but really – well, it *was* rather a surprise!

KHLYESTAKOV (*aside*). She's quite fetching herself – hm, hm, not bad at all . . . (*He shuffles towards her on his knees.*) Oh, Madame, Madame, can't you see that I'm dying of love!

ANNA. Oh, do get up, sir, the floor's filthy!

KHLYESTAKOV. No, no, on my knees . . . I must stay on my knees . . . 'til I hear my fate. . . . Is it to be life . . . or death?

ANNA. I don't know what you're carrying on about, really I don't. Are you making a declaration about my daughter?

KHLYESTAKOV. No, no, it's you I'm in love with, you! My whole life is at stake, for if you can't return my undying love then I'm not worthy of life at all! My heart is on fire as I beg for your hand . . . !

ANNA. But sir, I must point out that I am – er – in a manner of speaking – er – married.

KHLYESTAKOV. Married! What is marriage! True love knows

nothing of these formalities! As the poet said – ' 'Tis but itself the law condemns!'

ANNA. They do say 'True love can leap the fastest torrent,' don't they?

KHLYESTAKOV. Of course it can, beloved lady! We'll fly together, hand in hand, to the banks of some gurgling brook.... Your hand, I beg you, your hand!

Enter MARIA, *running.*

MARIA. Mamma, Pappa says you're to . . . (*She cries out as she sees* KHLYESTAKOV *on his knees.*) Well, what a surprise!

ANNA. What are you doing here, you little fidget, dashing in like a scalded cat, I thought I told you to keep out? What's a surprise, eh? I don't know what nonsense you've got in your head now, you're just like a child, no one would guess you were eighteen years old! [Won't you ever learn to behave like a properly brought-up young lady, haven't you got any manners at all?]

MARIA (*in tears*). But Mamma, I didn't know . . .

ANNA. You don't know nothing, that's your trouble, always in a whirl, just like those Lyapkin-Tyapkin girls, can't you find a better model than them? You could take your mother as an example, for instance, couldn't you?

KHLYESTAKOV (*taking* MARIA's *hand*). Anna Andreyevna, I beg you not to oppose our happiness! Give your blessing to our love!

ANNA (*astonished*). What? You mean – it's *her*?

Heavy winking from KHLYESTAKOV.

KHLYESTAKOV. Tell me quickly – is it life – or death?

ANNA (*turning on* MARIA). There, you see, you stupid girl? Just for the sake of a silly little baggage like you, His Excellency has to go down on his knees to me! And then of course you have to burst in like a lunatic . . . it would serve you right if I said no, just to teach you a lesson. You don't deserve such luck!

MARIA. I won't do it again, Mamma, I promise.

Enter MAYOR, *breathless.*

MAYOR. Your Excellency, mercy! Have mercy on me!

KHLYESTAKOV. Now what's the matter?

MAYOR. Those shopkeepers have been making complaints about me, I know they have, and it's all lies, not half of it's true, they're cheats and liars, the lot of them, they're always giving short measure and that. And that Sergeant's widow said I had her flogged; it's a rotten lie, she flogged herself!

KHLYESTAKOV. Oh, to hell with the Sergeant's widow, I've got other things to think about!

MARIA. Pappa, His Excellency has asked . . .

MAYOR. Don't you believe a word of it, Your Honour! They're just a pack of rotten liars! [A baby could see through them, the whole town knows what liars they are. And swindle – they'd swindle their own mothers out of half a kopek and boast about it, Your Honour!]

MARIA. Pappa, I think His Excellency wants to ask . . .

ANNA. Be quiet, girl! Do you know the honour Ivan Alexandrovich is doing us, my dear? He's asked for our daughter's hand in marriage!

MAYOR. What?! You're out of your mind, woman! Don't be angry with her, Your Excellency, she's a bit weak in the head. Her mother was just the same.

KHLYESTAKOV. But I really am asking your consent to my marrying your daughter. I love her!

MAYOR. I don't believe it.

ANNA. [But His Excellency is telling you!

KHLYESTAKOV. I'm quite serious. I'm going mad with love!

MAYOR. You must be joking.]

ANNA. God Almighty, what a fool the man is! His Excellency is *telling* you, dear!

MAYOR. I can't believe it.

KHLYESTAKOV. You must give us your consent! I'm desperate. I could do something awful if you refuse . . . and then my blood would be on your hands!

MAYOR. No, no, please, I'm innocent, I haven't done a thing; I swear it. . . . Yes, anything Your Excellency pleases. Oh, God! What am I saying? My head's going round! [I don't know what's happening . . . God a'mercy, I'm such a fool!]

ANNA. For pity's sake, give them your blessing, then!

> KHLYESTAKOV *approaches the* MAYOR, *leading* MARIA *by the hand.*

MAYOR. May God bless you both, I suppose, but none of it's my fault, I'm entirely innocent, you know.

> KHLYESTAKOV *kisses* MARIA. *The* MAYOR *is still puzzled.*

Hey, look, they're kissing each other!

> *The* MAYOR *rubs his eyes and stares.*

It's true! Is it true? It's true, they're engaged!

> *The* MAYOR *dances with joy.*

What about that, Anton! Three cheers for the Mayor! What a stroke of genius!

> *Enter* OSSIP.

OSSIP. The horses are ready, sir.

KHLYESTAKOV. Ah . . . right. Coming now.

MAYOR. What's that? Horses? Are you leaving?

KHLYESTAKOV. That's right.

MAYOR. But didn't I understand . . . ? Your Excellency was pleased to hint – er – possible marriage?

KHLYESTAKOV. Oh, I shan't be away a minute, well, that is, no more than a day . . . to see my uncle, you know, very rich uncle, have to get his blessing too, of course. I'll be back tomorrow.

MAYOR. We wouldn't presume to keep you, of course. We can only await the happiness of your return.

KHLYESTAKOV. That's right. Good. Well, I'll be back in no time. Goodbye, my darling . . . oh, I can't find words to express all I feel! Goodbye, beloved, my love, my darling, goodbye . . . (*He kisses* MARIA's *hand.*)

MAYOR. Is there nothing you need for the road, Your Excellency? You were a little short of ready money . . .

KHLYESTAKOV. No, no, what on earth made you think . . . (*Pause.*) Yes, well, perhaps I am – a bit short.

MAYOR. How much do you need?

KHLYESTAKOV. Let's see now, you lent me two hundred – no, of course, it was four, I mustn't take advantage of your mistake, must I? So if you could just let me have the same again, that would make a round eight hundred, wouldn't it?

MAYOR. Certainly, certainly! (*He produces notes.*) There, all in nice crisp new notes!

KHLYESTAKOV. Really! (*He takes the notes and examines them.*) Very nice, too. They say new banknotes bring you luck, don't they?

MAYOR. Indeed they do.

KHLYESTAKOV. Well, goodbye then, Anton Antonovich. Thanks for all your hospitality. I can say quite sincerely that I've never been so well received – anywhere, ever before, never! Goodbye, Anna Andreyevna! And farewell, my darling Maria Antonova! (KHLYESTAKOV *and* MARIA *go out together.*) My heart's joy! My angel! Goodbye!

MAYOR (*at the door*). Surely you're not riding in that dreadful public cart?

KHLYESTAKOV (*off*). Really, I prefer it. Springs make my head ache, you know.

DRIVER (*off*). Whoa-up!

MAYOR. At least let me get you something to sit on – a rug or something!

KHLYESTAKOV. What on earth for, it's nothing. (*Pause.*) Well, all right, if you insist.

MAYOR. Avdotya! Fetch a rug from the boxroom – the best one, the Persian rug with the blue border – hurry! (*He goes out.*)

DRIVER (*off*). Whoa!

MAYOR (*off*). When can we expect Your Excellency back?

KHLYESTAKOV (*off*). Tomorrow or the next day.

OSSIP (*off*). Is that our rug? All right, over here with it, tuck it round, that's right. Let's have some of that hay over here, then.

DRIVER (*off*). More hay here, no, over this side, you daft lump, that's it, now the rug, good. There you are, Your Excellency, you'll be nice and comfy.

KHLYESTAKOV (*off*). Goodbye, all! Goodbye, Anton Antonovich.

MAYOR (*off*). } Goodbye, Your Excellency.
MARIA (*off*). }

ANNA (*at window*). Goodbye, Ivan Alexandrovich!

KHLYESTAKOV (*off*). Goodbye, Mamma! Goodbye, Pappa!

DRIVER (*off*). Giddyap, giddyap!

The carriage bells ring into the distance.

The MAYOR *returns with* ANNA, *followed a moment later by* MARIA.

MAYOR. Aha, Anna, you never thought anything like this would happen, did you? A fine catch for your daughter, eh? Come on, admit it! [You never dreamed of such a thing, did you?] One moment you're just the wife of the Mayor and then, by damn! Suddenly you've got a young blood like that for a son-in-law!

ANNA. Nonsense, Anton, I knew it all along. It may be a surprise to you, but you're such a peasant, you've never mixed with decent people before.

MAYOR. Decent people! I'm decent people myself, [thank you!] Eh, but just think, Anna – what it does to us, we'll be flying high now, all right. (*He shouts off.*) Hey, you there! Come here! I'll fix that bunch of crooks! I'll teach 'em to come running with their complaints and petitions and that, they'll wish they'd never been born.

Enter the CONSTABLE.

Ah, it's you, Pugovitzin. Run and fetch those shopkeepers back here, sonny! By God, I'll fix that dirty pack of creeping Judases! [They're not going to get away with it this time, I'm going to make their lives hell, sheer burning hell! I want a list of everyone that came here to complain, everyone that signed a petition – yes, and the dirty scribblers who wrote out their petitions for them, put them all on the list!] See that everyone knows exactly how God has chosen to honour their Mayor. [Tell them he's not going to marry his daughter to any rotten common *ordinary* man, he's going to marry her to one of the grandest, one of the most powerful men in the whole world – a man such as they've never met, a man who can do anything, anything!] Tell them all! Shout it from the housetops, ring every bell in the town, damn it, make it a real celebration! Go on, hop it.

The CONSTABLE *goes off.*

So that's the way it's going to be. Well, Anna, where would you like to live – here, or in Petersburg?

ANNA. In Petersburg, of course! We couldn't possibly stay on here.

MAYOR. If you say Petersburg, my dear, Petersburg it shall be. Mind you, I'm not sure it wouldn't be just as nice to stay on here . . . it'll mean the end of my being Mayor, if we leave.

ANNA. I should think so too! There's not much to being a Mayor.

MAYOR. Hey! [D'you think I might get a high-up job in the Service, then, Anna?] With him being a personal friend of all the Ministers, and popping in and out of the Palace and that, he ought to get me promoted easy enough. Perhaps they'll make me a General! Eh, Anna? What do you think? Do you think they'll make me a General?

ANNA. I should hope so, I'm sure.

MAYOR. Dear God, I'd love to be a General! All those decorations across my chest [– which do you like best, Anna, the red for St Anne, or the blue of the White Eagle?

ANNA. The blue, of course.

MAYOR. Ha, you women, you always want the best! Even the red'd be nice, though. You know what's good about being a General, Anna? Everywhere you go there's] all those adjutants and couriers scurrying on ahead demanding the best horses for you. There won't be no horses for nobody else, but they'll have some for the General; the rest just have to wait their turn! . . . Councillors, Captains – yes – ha! And Mayors! They all have to wait! Ah! Those Mayors! Ha-ha! [You go to dine at the Governor's and all those Mayors – ha! they all have to stand up – ha-ha! – and bow – ha-ha! And you just ignore the whole rotten lot of them!] (*He doubles up with laughter and slaps his knees again and again.*) Yes, by damn, that's what I like about being a General!

ANNA. [I never heard anything so coarse, really! You've got to understand, Anton, our life's going to be completely different now, our friends won't be loud-mouthed judges who can't think about anything but shooting rabbits, they'll be counts and things, all sorts of society people with lovely refeened manners. In fact, Anton, I'm a bit worried about you – you sometimes come out with words and expressions that are *never* used in polite society!

MAYOR. Ah, to hell with that, words never did anyone any harm.

ANNA. Not when you're only a Mayor in a little country town, perhaps. But in Petersburg things are all very different, you know.

MAYOR. Yes, they say they serve a coulibiac of salmon that makes you faint at the first taste!

ANNA. A fine time to be talking about fish! In Petersburg . . . in Petersburg . . . we're going to have the finest house in town! I shall have my boudoir drenched in the finest perfume, so people will have to close their eyes in ecstasy as they come in . . . like this. (*She closes her eyes and sniffs, swooning.*)]

Enter the SHOPKEEPERS, *sheepishly.*

MAYOR. Aha, there you are, my fine friends!

SHOPKEEPERS (*all bowing low*). We wish you the best of health, Your Honour.

MAYOR. I bet you do! And how are you all, eh? How's business? Why, you tea-swillers, you counter-jumpers, you short-change merchants, so you thought you'd complain about me did you? You crooks, you creeping two-faced misbegotten store-rats! Scum! Well? Speak up. Where's it got you, eh? Thought you'd get me behind bars, did you? [The Devil blast you to hell and back you . . .

ANNA. Antosha! Language!

MAYOR (*vexed*). I can't worry about words now! (*To the* SHOPKEEPERS.*)] Did you know that Government Inspector you complained to is going to marry my daughter? Eh? Did you know that? What do you say to that? [By God, I'll show you, you're all swindlers, every one of you. (*He singles out* ABDULLIN.) You, you're a swindler. You make a hundred thousand on a Government contract by supplying shoddy material, then offer twenty yards of the same rubbish stuff to me and expect to get a medal for it! One word from me and you'd be – ah! Look at you, strutting about like turkey-cocks, thinking you're somebody! 'We're shopkeepers, we are, nobody can touch us, we're good as gentry any time, we are!' As if the gentry would . . . Ah! Pig-faces, what d'you know about gentry? At least they've got some manners, they got their hides tanned at school to some purpose, they know what's what. But you! You start off as swindlers and your masters beat you to teach you to swindle better! You learn how to give short measure before you've even learned the Lord's Prayer, and soon as your belly's fat enough and pockets full enough you start putting on airs! As if you were of the slightest significance to anyone! Just because you can empty a dozen samovars a day you think you're God's gift to Russia! Well, you're not. I don't give a damn for the whole pack of you!]

SHOPKEEPERS (*in chorus*). We're very sorry, Anton Antono-vich!

MAYOR. You want to complain, do you? (*Singling out* ABDULLIN.) Who was it let you charge twenty thousand for timber for building the bridge, when the stuff you supplied wasn't worth a hundred? Eh? Wasn't it me? Wasn't it? You nanny-goat, you! I suppose you'd forgotten that? I've only got to whisper and the whole lot of you'll be off to Siberia! [What about that, then, eh?]

ABDULLIN. Before God, Anton Antonovich, we're all very sorry! The Devil must have tempted us, your Honour. [We'll never do anything like that again, as God's our witness!] Ask for anything you like, anything . . . but please don't be angry with us!

MAYOR. [Don't be angry with you! Look at you crawling at my feet! And for why? Because I'm on top, that's why. And if things had happened to go the other way you'd be trampling me in the mud, you pigs, and throwing logs on top just to make sure! I know you!

SHOPKEEPERS (*bowing again*). Don't ruin us, Anton Antono-vich!]

MAYOR. Yes, it's 'Don't be angry with us' now, isn't it? But before, what was it before? (*He makes a menacing gesture.*) I'd like to . . . (*He stops, and shrugs.*) Well, I hope God forgives you, that's all. Lucky for you I'm not a vindictive man – but just you watch it from now on! My daughter isn't marrying some country yokel, remember – make sure your congratulations are appropriate – d'you understand? You'll not get away with a couple of salt cod and a barrel of sugar-lumps this time! [Now go on, off with the lot of you!]

The MAYOR *points to the door and the* SHOPKEEPERS *scurry out. Enter the* JUDGE *and the* CHARITY COMMISSIONER.

JUDGE. Anton Antonovich, my dear friend, is it really true? What a stroke of luck, eh?

CHARITY COMMISSIONER. Sincerest congratulations! I was delighted to hear of it, delighted! (*He crosses and kisses* ANNA's *hand.*) Anna Andreyevna! (*He crosses to kiss* MARIA's *hand.*) Maria Antonovna! Really delighted!

Enter RASTAKOVSKY.

RASTAKOVSKY. Anton Antonovich! Congratulations! May God give you long life, and the happy couple too! And crowds of grandchildren and great-grandchildren! Anna Andreyevna! (*He kisses her hand.*) Maria Antonovna! (*He kisses her hand.*)

Enter KOROBKIN *and* KOROBKIN's *wife.*

KOROBKIN. I must congratulate you, Anton Antonovich, I must! Anna Andreyevna. (*He kisses her hand.*) Maria Antonovna! (*He kisses her hand.*)

KOROBKIN'S WIFE (*slyly*). Most *sincere* congratulations, Anna Andreyevna, on your *marvellous* good fortune!

LYULYUKOV (*entering*). A thousand congratulations, Anna Andreyevna! (*He kisses her hand; turns and clicks his heels.*) Maria Antonovna, a thousand congratulations.

He is followed by hordes of guests, all offering congratulations and kissing hands. BOBCHINSKY *and* DOBCHINSKY *dash in, and push to the front.*

BOBCHINSKY. Allow me to congratulate you, Anton Antonovich!

DOBCHINSKY. Anton Antonovich, allow me to congratulate you on your good fortune!

BOBCHINSKY . . . on your good fortune!

DOBCHINSKY. Anna Andreyevna!

BOBCHINSKY. Anna Andreyevna!

They both try to kiss her hand at the same moment and knock their silly heads together.

DOBCHINSKY. Maria Antonovna! (*He kisses her hand.*) Allow me to congratulate you! I'm sure you'll be ever so happy, you'll wear dresses of gold and silver and drink the most wonderful soup [and live in a dream of pleasure!]

BOBCHINSKY (*interrupting*). Allow me, Maria Antonovna (*He kisses her hand.*) to congratulate you! I wish you all the wealth and happiness in the world – and a darling baby boy no bigger than this – (*He indicates the size.*) that you can hold in the palm of your hand! And what a noise the little rascal will make! (*He imitates a baby crying.*) Wah! Wah! Wah!

More GUESTS, *congratulations*, *kissing*, *the* SCHOOLS SUPERINTENDENT *and the* SCHOOLS SUPERINTEN-DENT'S WIFE *push through to the front.*

SCHOOLS SUPERINTENDENT. Allow me to congrat . . .

SCHOOLS SUPERINTENDENT'S WIFE (*running forward*). Ah, Anna Andreyevna, many congratulations, my dear! (*They kiss.*) I'm so happy and excited! 'Anna Andreyevna's daughter,' they told me, 'is going to marry that Government Inspector!' 'Heavens above,' I thought to myself. – and I was so pleased I ran straight to my husband. 'Luka,' I said, 'have you heard how lucky Anna Andreyevna's been?' So I told him. 'Thank God for that!' I thought to myself. And I said to Luka, 'Luka,' I said, 'I'm so happy, I can't wait to tell Anna Andreyevna how happy I am, she's always hoped for a good match for Maria, but *this* . . . she could hardly have dreamed.' Well, I was so happy I just cried, I couldn't say a word and Luka said, 'What on earth are you crying about?' and I said, 'Well, dear,' I said, 'I really don't know,' I said, and the tears just kept on coming and coming in torrents and Luka said . . .

G

MAYOR. Will you please all take a seat, Ladies and Gentlemen. (*Calling.*) Mishka! Bring some more chairs!

The GUESTS *seat themselves where they can.* MISHKA *brings chairs. Enter the* POLICE INSPECTOR *and a* CONSTABLE.

POLICE INSPECTOR. Allow me to congratulate Your Honour and wish you all prosperity and a long life!

MAYOR. Thank you, thank you. Do sit down, please.

JUDGE. Aren't you going to tell us how it all happened, Anton Antonovich, right from the beginning?

MAYOR. Well, it was a very funny business. His Excellency actually did the proposing himself . . .

ANNA (*taking it off him*). . . . in such a charming way, so gentle and considerate he was! Oh it was really lovely, the way he spoke! ['Anna Andreyevna,' he said, 'It's all due to your own exquisite virtues,' he said – oh it's lovely to have dealings with a real gentleman like that!] 'Believe me, Anna Andreyevna,' he said, 'my own life means nothing to me,' he said, 'I'm doing this purely out of regard for your own amazing qualities . . .'

MARIA. Oh Mamma, it was me he said that to!

ANNA. [Hold your tongue, girl, you know nothing about it, can't you learn not to interfere?] 'Anna Andreyevna,' he said to me, 'you're an astonishing woman,' he said. Oh, he said such lovely flattering things I can't tell you! [And then when I said we couldn't really hope for such an honour,] he fell right down on his knees in front of me [– really it was touching to see him!] And he said, 'Anna Andreyevna, [please don't make me unhappy,] say you respond to my feelings or I shall kill myself!'

MARIA. But really, Mamma, he was saying that about *me*!

ANNA. Well, I suppose it was about you as well, I never said it wasn't.

MAYOR. He quite frightened us, you know. 'My blood will be on your hands,' he kept saying.

ALL. No!
    Never!

Fancy that!

He never did!

SCHOOLS SUPERINTENDENT. It's the hand of destiny.

CHARITY COMMISSIONER. [Rubbish, destiny hasn't got any hands.] Nonsense. It's the just reward of true merit, that's what it is. (*Aside.*) The dirtiest pigs always root up the biggest acorns.

JUDGE. Anton Antonovich, you can have that puppy, you know, if you really want it.

MAYOR. I can't be bothered with puppies now.

JUDGE. You can have any one you like – take your pick!

KOROBKIN'S WIFE. [*Dearest* Anna Andreyevna,] I'm so *pleased* at your wonderful *luck*!

KOROBKIN. But where's the distinguished guest, then? Didn't someone tell me he'd left town?

MAYOR. Yes, he's gone off for a day or two on important business—

ANNA. —to visit his rich uncle and ask his blessing.

MAYOR. —ask his blessing, but he'll be back tomorrow or the – Asssssssssstishoooo! (*He sneezes – there is a general chorus of 'Bless you'!*) Thank you – tomorrow or the – AAAAAAA-TISHOOOOO! (*General blessings, some of them very loud.*) Thank you.

POLICE INSPECTOR. Good health to Your Honour!

BOBCHINSKY. May you live a hundred years and have a sack full of gold!

DOBCHINSKY. May you live over a hundred years and have several sacks of gold!

JUDGE (*aside*). Hope you die of the plague!

DOBCHINSKY'S WIFE (*aside*). May you burn in hell!

MAYOR. Thank you, thank you! And I wish you all the same!

ANNA. Of course, we shall be living in Petersburg, now. I'm afraid I find it awfully – provincial, here – not at all congenial. And my husband, of course (*She shrugs.*) will become a General.

MAYOR. I don't mind admitting I rather fancy being a General!

SCHOOLS SUPERINTENDENT. God grant you become one then!

RASTAKOVSKY (*aside*). To God, anything is possible!

JUDGE. Big ships must sail in deep waters!

CHARITY COMMISSIONER. And honours fall to the honourable!

JUDGE (*aside*). If they make him a general, it'll be like putting a saddle on a cow. [Still, he's not there yet, thank God. There's better men than him that aren't generals yet.]

CHARITY COMMISSIONER (*aside*). You never know; he might make it. He's conceited enough for it already. (*To the* MAYOR). You won't forget us, though, will you, Anton Antonovich?

JUDGE. If anything happened to go wrong here – you know, trouble – you'd help us, wouldn't you?

KOROBKIN. My son goes to Petersburg next year, to enter the service. I hope you'll keep an eye on the poor lad?

MAYOR. Of course, of course, I'll do everything I can, you know me.

ANNA. You're always much too ready to make promises, Antosha. You're not going to have time for little things like that. Anyway, why should you?

MAYOR. Why not, my dear? There's always time for helping a friend.

ANNA. I daresay, but you needn't go around promising to help every fool in the place.

KOROBKIN'S WIFE (*aside to the* SCHOOLS SUPERINTENDENT'*s* WIFE). Did you hear that? That's what she thinks of us!

SCHOOLS SUPERINTENDENT'S WIFE (*aside*). She's always been like that, the stupid bitch. No tact. Spit in her eye and she'll say it's the dew from heaven.

Enter the POSTMASTER, *waving a letter.*

POSTMASTER. Listen, all of you, listen, I've got some terrible news. The man we took for a Government Inspector wasn't the Inspector at all!

ALL. What!
     Not the Inspector!

Not the Government Inspector!

POSTMASTER. Not the Government Inspector at all! It's all in this letter!

MAYOR. What letter?

POSTMASTER. This letter! One he wrote himself. It was brought down to my office, and I saw it was addressed to someone in Post Office Street, Petersburg, so of course I thought, 'Dear God, he's sending in a report about me.' So of course I opened it, to see.

MAYOR. How could you do such a thing!

POSTMASTER. I don't know myself, I really don't – there seemed to be a supernatural force egging me on. [I was just going to send it off, express, when suddenly I was seized by a curiosity stronger than anything I'd ever known before. I felt I couldn't do it, I couldn't open it, but all the time something was compelling me to break the seal! In one ear there was a voice whispering, 'Don't touch that seal, you'll be in trouble if you do,' but then in the other ear another voice, even stronger, was saying, 'Go on, break the seal, open it up!' And soon as I touch that wax, seemed my blood was afire, and when I open up the letter, I was all ice, trembling all over and nearly fainting!]

MAYOR. How dare you open a letter from such an important personage!

POSTMASTER. Aha, that's just it, Anton Antonovich, he's not important at all! He isn't a personage, either!

MAYOR. What is he, then?

POSTMASTER. He's nothing, a nobody! I don't know what you could call him.

MAYOR (angrily). [What the devil do you mean?] How dare you call him a nobody! I'll have you arrested!

POSTMASTER. Who? You?

MAYOR. Yes. me!

POSTMASTER. You wouldn't do that.

MAYOR. Wouldn't I? Do you realize he's going to marry my daughter? I'll be a personage myself then, and I'll have you packed off to Siberia if you don't watch it.

POSTMASTER. You don't want to be talking about Siberia,

Anton Antonovich! Siberia's a long way off. I best read you the letter, I think, shall I read it out, then?

ALL. Yes, yes!

Read it!

Read us the letter!

POSTMASTER. Right, then. Hrchm. 'My dear Tyapichkin, Extraordinary things have been happening to me. On my way home I was completely cleaned out by a very sharp infantry officer, so there I was, holed up in the wretched little inn here and being threatened by the innkeeper because I couldn't pay my bill when suddenly – I suppose because of my Petersburg clothes and looks – I found the whole town had mistaken me for some Government Inspector, [and everything changed completely!] Here I am now, living a life of luxury in the Mayor's house, flirting with his wife and daughter both at the same time! I haven't made up my mind yet which I'll go for first – the wife's probably the best bet, she looks as if she's ready for anything! [Remember the days when we were so hard up we had to live on our wits, and the time that confectioner threw us out on our necks because I'd told him to "book those pies to the King of England's account"! It's a bit different here, I can tell you!] They're all falling over themselves to lend me money – as much as I ask for! Honestly, you'd die laughing, they're such nitwits! I know you write bits and pieces for the theatre sometimes – you really ought to put this lot in a play, it would be a riot! First there's the Mayor, you can see at a glance he's a crook – though not a very clever one . . .'

MAYOR. Rubbish! I don't believe that's there!

POSTMASTER (*showing him the letter*). See for yourself.

MAYOR (*reading*). '. . . crook . . . not a very clever . . .' You must have written that in yourself!

POSTMASTER. Don't be silly, how could I?

CHARITY COMMISSIONER. Oh, read on!

POSTMASTER (*reading again*). 'The Mayor . . . see at a glance he's a crook . . .'

MAYOR. Dammit, you don't have to keep repeating it! We've all heard that bit!

POSTMASTER. Mm . . . Mmmmmmm . . . a . . . not a very clever one '. . . The Postmaster – er – the Postmaster's a good enough fellow . . .' (*Pause.*) Well, there's something a bit rude [about me] here, I'll go on to . . .

MAYOR. No, no, read it!

POSTMASTER. Why should I?

MAYOR. If you're supposed to be reading the letter, get on and read it – all of it!

CHARITY COMMISSIONER. Here, let me read it. (*He takes the letter, puts on his spectacles and reads.*) 'The Postmaster's a half-blind half-wit, though he's sharp enough to tamper with the mail when he feels like it . . .'

POSTMASTER (*to the listeners*). The young scamp! [He ought to be whipped!]

CHARITY COMMISSIONER. Hm! (*Reading.*) 'Then there's the Charity Comm – Comm – Comm—' (*He stops.*)

KOROBKIN. What's stopping you now?

CHARITY COMMISSIONER. It's – er – a bit difficult to read. You can see he's a proper rascal, though.

KOROBKIN (*trying to take the letter*). Give it here, my eyes are better than yours.

CHARITY COMMISSIONER. No, it's all right. I'll read it. It's legible enough further on.

POSTMASTER. No, let's hear it all, we've had it all so far!

ALL. Give it to him!
    Let him have it!
    Let Korobkin read it!

CHARITY COMMISSIONER. Oh, all right, [here you are. There, look, you begin there.] (*He covers part of the letter with his fingers.*)
    They all crowd round, exclaiming.

POSTMASTER. No, come on, now, read the whole thing!

KOROBKIN (*removing the* CHARITY COMMISSIONER'*s hand*). 'The Charity Commissioner, Zemlyanika, looks just like—' it's quite easy to read – 'just like a pig in a wig . . .'

CHARITY COMMISSIONER. Really! It's not even funny! Whoever heard of a pig in a wig! (*He shrugs.*)

KOROBKIN (*reading*). 'The Schools Superintendent can't

speak for twitching – he's frightened of his own shadow . . .'

SCHOOLS SUPERINTENDENT. What does he mean, t-t-twitch-t-twitching . . . ?

JUDGE (*aside*). Nothing about me so far, thank God!

KOROBKIN (*reading*). 'The Judge . . .'

JUDGE. Look here, this letter's far too long, it's getting boring, [What's the point in listening to all this rubbish?]

SCHOOLS SUPERINTENDENT. Oh, no, you don't!

POSTMASTER. Go on reading. We might as well hear it all, now.

KOROBKIN (*reading*). 'The Judge, Lyapkin-Tyapkin, thinks so much about his dogs that he's beginning to look like one!'

JUDGE. Well, there's nothing wrong in looking like a dog! Some dogs are very beautiful!

KOROBKIN (*reading*). ['On the whole, though, they're quite a friendly, good-hearted bunch.] I'll say goodbye now, old chap. I've decided to follow your example and devote myself to literature, my life's getting to be an awful bore and one really ought to do something about nourishing the intellect. [I'm beginning to feel I ought to devote myself to some of the higher things of life.] Write to me [at Podkatilovka] in Saratov. Your old friend, Ivan Alexandrovich Khlyestakov.' [(*He turns over the letter and reads the address.*) It's addressed to: Ivan Vassilyevich, Ninety-seven, first on the right through the courtyard, third floor, Post Office Street, Saint Petersburg.]

KOROBKIN'S WIFE. Oh, but it's all so dreadful!

MAYOR. This is going to kill me. I'm starting to die already. Oh, my eyes, my eyes, something's happening to my eyes. . . . All I can see are pigs' snouts, pigs' snouts everywhere! Where is he? Bring him back! Bring him back!

POSTMASTER. How can we bring him back? I told them to give him the fastest horses we've got [and God knows why but I gave him a note to the other posting stations to give him their best horses too!

KOROBKIN'S WIFE. What a mess it all is.] I've never known anything like it!

JUDGE (*wailing*). But I lent him three hundred roubles!

POSTMASTER. So did I!

SCHOOLS SUPERINTENDENT. So did I!

CHARITY COMMISSIONER. I lent him four hundred!

BOBCHINSKY. And Peter Ivanovich and I lent him sixty-five between us!

JUDGE (*spreading his hands*). But how did it happen!? That's what I want to know! How could we make such a stupid mistake?

MAYOR (*striking his forehead*). Oh, God, how could I be such a fool. I must be losing my wits in my old age! Thirty years I've been in public service, and no one's ever got the better of me! I've beaten the worst swindlers [in the country] at their own game. I've cheated cheats who could have cheated the whole human race out of immortality! I've bamboozled three Governors in a row . . . (*He waves his hand dismissively.*) [. . . as if Governors were anything to worry about . . .]

ANNA. But it's impossible, Antosha! [After all,] he's engaged to Maria!

   MARIA *weeps.*

MAYOR (*furious*). Engaged! [Bah! Don't you give me your 'engaged'!] (*In a frenzy.*) Look at me – come on – look! Every Christian and heathen and savage in the world – come and have a look at the Mayor, look at the fool he's made of himself! Fool! (*He shakes his fist at himself.*) Taking that jumped-up little worm, [that bag of rubbish,] for a personage! Think of him bowling along now, with all his bells a-jingle, laughing his blasted head off! He'll tell his dirty little tale all over Russia. I shall be a laughing-stock. Some inky little scribbler'll put us all in a play, yes, every one of you! That'll hurt, I promise you! He won't spare us – rank, position, appearance, anything to make an audience snigger, it'll all go in! (*He suddenly turns on the audience.*) What do you think you're laughing at, eh?! You're laughing at yourselves, do you know that? Ah, what's the use? (*Sudden access of fury; he dances with rage.*) I'd like to get my hands on all those writers, damned snivelling liberals, the lot of you! I'd grind you into a jelly and kick you to hell and gone, you filthy parasites! (*He grinds all writers under his heel.*)

Pause.

[I'm not thinking straight. Those whom the Gods wish to punish, they first drive mad. Very true in my case!] (*Pause.*) What was there about that little tick that made us take him for a Government Inspector? Eh? What was there? Not that much! (*He measures off the tip of his finger.*) But there you all were, buzzing around, crying 'The Inspector, it's the Inspector, it must be the Inspector.' Well? Whose idea was it first, eh? Tell me that! (*He glares round.*)

CHARITY COMMISSIONER. For the life of me, I can't remember. [I can't seem to think straight, either.]

JUDGE. I'll tell you who started it! It was those two! (*He points to* BOBCHINSKY *and* DOBCHINSKY.)

BOBCHINSKY. It wasn't me! It never crossed my mind!

DOBCHINSKY. I didn't have anything to do with it!

CHARITY COMMISSIONER. Yes, it was! Of course it was those two!

SCHOOLS SUPERINTENDENT. That's right, they came scampering in here straight from the Inn like a pair of lunatics. 'He's here, he's here already! He won't part with any money! It must be him!' A fine bird you chose, the two of you!

MAYOR. Oh, yes, you nosey parkers, it would be you, wouldn't it? The town gossips!

CHARITY COMMISSIONER. To hell with them!

MAYOR. [All you two blockheads can do is snoop around town getting everyone into a tangle with your daft tales! You're a fine pair of boobies, aren't you.]

JUDGE. Bunglers!

SCHOOLS SUPERINTENDENT. Thick-heads!

CHARITY COMMISSIONER. Pot-bellied pair of idiots!

Everyone crowds round, accusing them.

BOBCHINSKY. It wasn't me, really it wasn't. It was Peter Ivanovich, who first . . .

DOBCHINSKY. No, no, Peter Ivanovich, it was you who said it first . . .

BOBCHINSKY. It wasn't me, you were the first, you were the first . . .

Enter a GENDARME *in splendid uniform.*

GENDARME (*announces superbly*). The Government Inspector from Saint Petersburg has arrived, with instructions from the Tsar. He demands your immediate attendance at the Inn.

Tableau of consternation.

CURTAIN

Methuen's Modern Plays

EDITED BY JOHN CULLEN AND GEOFFREY STRACHAN

Methuen Playscripts